MYTH AND REALITY
IN THE OLD TESTAMENT

STUDIES IN BIBLICAL THEOLOGY

MYTH AND REALITY
IN THE
OLD TESTAMENT

BREVARD S. CHILDS
Yale University Divinity School

SCM PRESS LTD
56 BLOOMSBURY STREET
LONDON

FIRST PUBLISHED 1960
SECOND EDITION 1962
PRINTED IN GREAT BRITAIN BY
W. & J. MACKAY & CO LTD, CHATHAM

CONTENTS

Contents

PREFACE TO THE FIRST EDITION

This book is written in the conviction that the problem of myth in the Old Testament is essentially the problem of the Old Testament's understanding of reality. The thesis developed is that myth and the Old Testament have as their ultimate concern an understanding of reality; however, their concepts are at variance with one another. Because of a new understanding of the redemptive activity of God, the Old Testament developed a concept of reality which came into conflict with the mythical. There followed a struggle in which the Old Testament attempted to alter the form of myth so as to be able to use it for its own witness.

The development of this thesis begins with the problem of defining myth and determining its function in the understanding of reality. The writer then attempts to show the conflict of the myth with the Old Testament's concept of reality and how the conflict is solved. This is done on the basis of a close exegetical study of several typical passages. This evidence leads to an investigation of the categories of Old Testament thinking concerning time and space in which the contrast to the mythical is demonstrated. Finally, on the basis of this study the theological problem of myth and its relation to the Old Testament's understanding of reality is discussed.

Many of the basic problems of Biblical theology are at stake in this study. In recent times we have heard much about revelation within the Bible being communicated not in the form of ideas but as event. It has become a common practice to speak about God's acting in history. We hear much about Old Testament revelation as a *Heilsgeschichte* (history of redemption). However, it appears that confusion exists as to the exact nature of 'event' and of 'history'. Bultmann criticizes Cullmann for his failure to define precisely his use of the word *Heilsgeschichte*: 'I cannot recognize that for him there is any difference in the meaning of the term history as applied to the "history of redemption" (*Heilsge schichte*) and history as "world history" (*Weltgeschichte*)'.[1] This study attempts a clarification of the term 'history' in relation to the Old Testament and its function as a medium of Biblical reality.

Then again, the problem of myth itself has taken on a new importance in our time. In fact, one should almost offer a defence for another monograph on the subject. While Bultmann's pro gramme has been constantly held in mind, this book offers a dif ferent approach to the problem, while at the same time it con cerns itself almost exclusively with the Old Testament. Neverthe less, in spite of this divergence there is the common concern with the problem of myth and reality.

Finally, the author hopes to make a contribution to the under standing of the unusual thought-patterns involved in Hebrew mentality. Great strides have been made by recent scholarship in demonstrating the need of ridding ourselves of Western pre suppositions in reading the Bible. In treating the subjects of time and space there has been a conscious effort to allow the Old Testament its full freedom of expression. The Biblical concept of time especially continues to suffer under the restraints of histori cism. This monograph tries to take history seriously, yet at the same time to resist the inroads of foreign categories which are vestiges of a peculiar philosophy of history.

The formation of this book has passed through various stages. Originally the subject of myth in the Old Testament was the subject of a doctoral thesis. Since the completion of the thesis in 1954, the material has been thoroughly revised on two occasions and this has resulted in a completely new book.

I should like to express my appreciation to the many who have been instrumental in my development along with the book. I should particularly like to thank my professors, Dr Walter Baum gartner and Dr Walther Eichrodt, who guided me into the subject and gave much of their time. I am grateful for the stimulus of two

[1]R. Bultmann, 'Heilsgeschichte und Geschichte,' *TLZ* (1948), p. 662.

German friends, Wilhelm Wilkens and Georg Sauer, and I should like to thank my colleague, Frederick Herzog, for invaluable insights, especially over the last three years. I appreciate the encouragement of Professor G. Ernest Wright, along with his many helpful comments. I am also indebted to Professor H. H. Rowley for reading the manuscript.

This book is dedicated to my wife, Ann, who has lived with myth for over three years and has remained unfailing in support.

B.S.C.

Plymouth, Wisconsin,
October, 1957

PREFACE TO THE SECOND EDITION

I have used the occasion of a new edition to bring the bibliography up-to-date with the addition of a considerable amount of recent literature. I have also made minor changes in the text. However, the argument of the book remains the same.

B.S.C.

New Haven, Conn.,
October, 1961

LIST OF ABBREVIATIONS

AO	*Archiv für Orient-Forschung*
AJSL	*American Journal of Semitic Languages and Literatures*
ANET	*Ancient Near-Eastern Texts relating to the Old Testament* (2nd ed., 1955), ed. Pritchard
AOT	*Altorientalische Texte zum A. T.* (2nd ed., 1926), ed. Gressmann
BASOR	*Bulletin of the American Schools of Oriental Research*
BH	*Biblia Hebraica* (3rd ed., 1937), ed., R. Kittel
BZAW	Beihefte zur *ZAW*
CBQ	*The Catholic Biblical Quarterly*
ERE	*Encyclopaedia of Religion and Ethics,* ed. J. Hastings
EvTh	*Evangelische Theologie*
EVV	English versions
HUCA	*Hebrew Union College Annual*
IEJ	*Israel Exploration Journal*
JAOS	*Journal of the American Oriental Society*
JBL	*Journal of Biblical Literature*
JCS	*Journal of Cuneiform Studies*
JNES	*Journal of Near Eastern Studies*
JPOS	*Journal of the Palestine Oriental Society*
JQR	*The Jewish Quarterly Review*
JSS	*The Journal of Semitic Studies*
KeDo	*Kerygma und Dogma*
LXX	The Septuagint
MT	Masoretic Text
MVAG	*Mitteilungen der Vorderasiatischen (Vorderasiatisch-Ägyptischen) Gesellschaft*
RB	*Revue biblique*
RGG	*Die Religion in Geschichte und Gegenwart* (2nd ed.)
RHPR	*Revue d'histoire et de philosophie religieuses*
RHR	*Revue de l'Histoire des Religions*

List of Abbreviations

TLZ	*Theologische Literaturzeitung*
TR	*Theologische Rundschau*
TWNT	*Theologisches Wörterbuch zum Neuen Testament*
TZ	*Theologische Zeitschrift*
VT	*Vetus Testamentum*
ZAW	*Zeitschrift für die alttestamentliche Wissenschaft*
ZTK	*Zeitschrift für Theologie und Kirche*

I

THE PROBLEM OF A DEFINITION
OF MYTH

It is not our purpose to review the long history which led to the modern understanding of myth.[1] We are consciously limiting the discussion to the definition of myth as it has been used in the history of modern *Biblical* scholarship. Within this field there have been developed two main approaches to the understanding of myth which differ in decisive points from each other. Naturally, there are countless variations within each classification, but these do not obscure the broad lines which we are sketching. Much of the misunderstanding concerning the term 'myth' in recent years has resulted from the failure to specify how the term is being used. For clarity's sake we will characterize these two lines of interpretation as the 'broad' and the 'narrow' definitions of myth and deal with them respectively.

1. Our understanding of the historical rise of the broad definition of the myth has been greatly enhanced by the thorough study of Hartlich and Sachs.[2] They pointed out that the term 'myth' received its first precise formulation in modern times from the classical philologist, C. G. Heyne, who defined the myth as a necessary and universal form of expression within the early stage of man's intellectual development, in which unexplainable events were attributed to the direct intervention of the gods.[3] His concept of the myth was soon applied to the Old Testament by the so-called 'mythical school' (Eichhorn, Gabler, G. L. Bauer), and

[1]Cf. Jan de Vries, *Forschungsgeschichte der Mythologie* (München, 1961), for survey of the history of research.
[2]C. Hartlich and W. Sachs, *Der Ursprung des Mythosbegriffes in der modernen Bibelwissenschaft* (Tübingen, 1952).
[3]*Ibid.*, pp. 12 ff.

finally to the New Testament by D. F. Strauss. In contemporary scholarship this definition has been defended by R. Bultmann.[1] A clear statement of the broad definition of myth is offered by Hartlich and Sachs:

> The mythical movement treats principally on the same level all statements concerning miraculous and supernatural occurrences especially of a direct miraculous intervention or appearance of the deity as well as any other supernatural being. It designates them uniformly as 'mythical' in so far as the statements concerning such events arise from a pre-scientific and uncritical, naïve stage of consciousness, regardless of whether they appear in the Bible or other religious documents.[2]

In analysing the broad definition of myth it is important to note at the outset that this is not a phenomenological but a historic-philosophical definition. It stems directly from the philosophical distinction between the supernatural and the natural which becomes the criterion for classifying all material. From the modern scientific perspective a critical evaluation of the material is offered. The danger of such an approach is that false categories, unsuitable to the subject, are forced upon it. It means approaching the myth through the eyes of the critical Western mind and restricting from the beginning the kind of reality which the myth can contain. This is a fundamental error of rationalism. Moreover the phenomenon of myth in this definition has not been approached as a totality, but the mythical has been relegated to the sphere of the supernatural. However, the supernatural elements of the myth do not stand isolated; they are intimately connected with a total understanding of reality. The definition thereby fails to do justice to the inner coherence of mythical thinking. By focusing on a false distinction it has overlooked the actual purpose of the myth. Finally, the broad definition is not a useful tool for Biblical studies since it obscures many important distinctions. To classify every expression of the supernatural as mythical

---

[1]*Kerygma and Myth*, ed. H. W. Bartsch (London, 1953), p. 10: 'Mythology is the use of imagery to express the other-wordly in terms of this world and the divine in terms of human life, the other side in terms of this side.'

[2]Hartlich-Sachs, *op. cit.*, p. 148.

destroys the real distinctions between the saga, the legend, and the myth, all of which share in supernatural events.

2. The 'narrow' or 'form-critical' definition of myth deviates radically from the broad definition. This concept of myth stems originally from the work of the Grimm brothers who in the preface to their *Kinder- und Hausmärchen* (1812) defined the myth as a literary form concerning stories of gods, which was to be distinguished from other literary types such as the legend and fairy tale. The analysis of the historical development of myth as a literary type was later corrected by Wundt;[1] however, the Grimms' definition remained basic. This understanding of myth, which in turn entered Biblical research, is well summarized by Gunkel: 'Myths . . . are stories about gods. They are to be distinguished from sagas where the active persons are human.'[2] It is instructive to contrast the two adjacent articles on the subject of myth written by Gunkel and Bultmann[3] and to see the widely varying usage of the term. The narrow definition arose from a need to define a certain form of prose more precisely, both in its literary and pre-literary stage. It belongs to the science of description and offers no philosophical evaluation of the material.

While this definition has proved very useful in Biblical research, it is inadequate to form the basis for our study of myth in the Old Testament. In the first place, myth is defined too exclusively as a literary product. Although its pre-literary stage is evident to those applying it, nevertheless, the function of the definition is directed primarily to defining limits on the literary plane. It is not helpful in understanding the function of the myth within the total thinking of a culture. The definition remains on the formal level without attempting to penetrate to the essence of the myth. Secondly, there has been a tendency among those using this definition to fail to see the essential problem of myth in the Old Testament. If myth is understood only as a 'story of gods', then there is no true myth possible in a monotheistic religion, and myth is eliminated

---

[1]W. Wundt, *Völkerpsychologie*, V (2nd ed., Leipzig, 1914–20), pp. 31 ff.
[2]H. Gunkel, *Genesis* (4th ed., Göttingen, 1917), p. xiv; *RGG*, IV (1927–2), pp. 363 ff.
[3]*RGG*, IV, pp. 382 ff. and 390 ff.

by definition from the Old Testament.[1] The defenders of this definition have often failed to reckon with the possibility that the Old Testament faith may have maintained and even developed mythical thinking while merely eliminating the crude polytheism. The problem of the basic understanding of reality contained in the myth and its relation to Biblical faith has not been adequately touched upon in this definition.

3. In the light of the above criticism it is our contention that the definition of myth should be first of all a *phenomenological* one if it is to be a useful tool for Biblical research. This means that we do not consider a philosophical, historical, form-critical, or aesthetic definition of myth the correct starting point for discussing the problem of myth in the Old Testament. Moreover, we feel that there does exist among scholars of comparative religion a general consensus of opinion regarding the phenomenological definition of myth. It is this consensus which we will attempt to sketch briefly in the next chapter.

[1] A. Weiser, *Einleitung in das Alte Testament* (2nd ed., Göttingen, 1949), p. 5
[ET of 4th ed. (London. 1961), p. 57.]

II

MYTH AS AN UNDERSTANDING
OF REALITY

A. THE ESSENCE OF MYTH[1]

The myth is an expression of man's understanding of reality. It stems from a thought pattern which differs in decisive points from the modern critical one. This is especially true in regard to the manner in which the world is conceived. Whereas the man of critical mind thinks of the world about him as passive and impersonal, the primitive man conceives of his surroundings as active and living, with powers which influence every area of his life. The activity of these powers in nature is perceived by him in the manifold impressions of nature which force themselves vividly upon him. Corresponding to his intimate contact with nature there is an unusual quality of openness and receptivity to these impinging powers. The growth and decay of his fruit tree, the birth and death of his family, the rise and setting of the sun, are the overwhelming signs of a reality which determines his life. To these impressions from nature as material for myth must also be

---

[1] The summary account of this complex problem is not meant to obscure the difficulty of the subject. Because of the nature of our investigation, we are forced to draw some general lines and then make reference to important literature for those wishing a more detailed study of the problem. E. B. Tylor, *Primitive Culture*, I (2nd ed., London, 1873), pp. 273 ff.; W. Wundt, *Völkerpsychologie,* IV (2nd ed., Leipzig, 1914–20), pp. 3 ff. and V, VI; P. Ehrenreich, *Die allgemeine Mythologie* (Leipzig, 1910), pp. 59 ff.; L. Lévy-Bruhl, *La Mentalité Primitive* (14me ed., Paris, 1947), pp. 17 ff.; J. W. Hauer, *Die Religionen* (Stuttgart, 1923), pp. 340 ff.; L. Lévy-Bruhl, *La Mythologie Primitive* (Paris, 1935); H. Frankfort, ed., *The Intellectual Adventure of Ancient Man* (Chicago, 1948), pp. 3 ff.; C. Kerényi, *Introduction to a Science of Mythology* (1951); E. Buess, *Geschichte des mythischen Erkennens* (München, 1953), pp. 06 ff; M. Eliade, *Patterns in Comparative Religion* (ET, New York, 1958), pp. 410 ff.; *Myth. A Symposium*, ed. T. Sebeok (Bloomington, 1958); Y. Kaufmann, *The Religion of Israel* (ET, Chicago, 1960), pp. 21 ff.

included the whole mass of psychological stimuli arising from the human subconscious, such as dreams, hallucinations, etc., which, for the primitive man, possess an objectivity similar to that of the world about him. The moment of seizure (*Ergriffenheit*), in which he is captivated by an impinging reality, is the first presupposition for the formation of the myth.

Essential in the process of formation is the creative spirit of man. He attempts to order the multiplicity of impressions into an intelligible and unified whole. In the plastic form of the myth a principle of organization is found which creates out of the chaos of particulars a unity. The unique character of the myth is found in the fact that the shaping of this raw material takes place on the plane of personalized powers in which the elemental impressions of nature are transformed into stories of gods.[1]

The man of the mythical world never sees the world order as a condition to be taken for granted, but always as something in the process of becoming. The structure of the world cannot be reckoned as given data, but as the transitory effect of events which must constantly be recharged with energy. 'Mythical thinking presupposes that this condition (the present world order) is an occurrence (*Gewordenes*), a work of creative powers, which from the world of chaos—or at least a false order—created the existing order.'[2] Precisely at this point a decisive element in the nature of myth is seen: In order to understand the structure of being of the present world as an occurrence, myth projects the establishment of this order back to an event in the primeval age.[3] It conceives of the present reality which impinges upon the senses as having its true basis in a primeval event which determines the present world structure. Malinowski expresses it as follows: 'Myth . . . in its living primitive form, is not merely a story told but a reality lived

[1]For a discussion of the problem of how the idea of gods developed Tylor, *op. cit.*, pp. 273 ff.; Wundt, *op. cit.*, VI, pp. 1 ff.; N. Söderblom, *Das Werden des Gottesglaubens* (Leipzig, 1916), pp. 114 ff.; R. Otto, *Gottheit und Gottheiten der Arier* (Giessen, 1932), pp. 16 ff.; G. van der Leeuw, *Religion in Essence and Manifestation* (London, 1938), pp. 23 ff.

[2]Ad. E. Jensen, *Mythos und Kult bei Naturvölkern* (2nd ed., Wiesbaden, 1960) p. 79.

[3]*Ibid.*, p. 64.

It is not of the nature of fiction . . . but it is a living reality, believed to have once happened in primeval times, and continuing ever since to influence the world and human destinies.'[1] One recognizes this reference to an occurrence in the distant past in such typical expressions of the myth as 'when above the heaven was not named', or 'in the days of yore, the days when the sky had been separated', or 'in the beginning was Ju-ok the great creator'.

We have seen the connexion of the myth to a primeval event as being determinative for the present structure of reality, but this is only one side of mythical thinking. The modern study of the myth has demonstrated in a most convincing manner the close connexion of myth with cult.[2] In the drama of the cult an actualization of the original cosmic events takes place in which that which once occurred is again realized *hic et nunc*. The reality of the mythical, timeless event enters into the present moment of time. As in the primeval age, the participant shares directly in the elemental powers of the creation. In the cultic drama he partakes of the power of the primeval age which is loosed from all time sequence. 'Everything is just as it was on that first day.'[3] By anchoring itself to the distant primeval event, the myth attempts to express the enduring nature of the world of being. It functions as the bearer of the cult since the cult possesses only a punctual

[1] B. Malinowski, 'Myth in Primitive Psychology', *Magic, Science and Religion* (New York, 1954), p. 100.

[2] The relation of the myth to the cult is extremely complex. The problem was clearly formulated by W. Robertson Smith, *The Religion of the Semites* (rev. ed., London, 1894), pp. 18 ff.; cf. the further discussion in Wundt, *op. cit.,* V, pp. 20 ff.; S. Mowinckel, *Psalmenstudien,* II (Kristiania, 1922), pp. 19 ff.; van der Leeuw, *Religion in Essence* (1938), pp. 373 ff.; *Myth and Ritual,* ed. S. H. Hooke (London, 1933); *Labyrinth,* ed. S. H. Hooke (1935); W. F. Otto, *Dionysos, Mythos und Kultus* (Frankfort, 1933); C. Kluckholm, *Harvard Theol. Review,* 35 (1942), pp. 45 ff.; S. Mowinckel, *Religion og Kultus* (Oslo, 1950); T. H. Gaster, *Thespis* (2nd ed., Garden City, 1961), pp. 23 ff.; Gaster, *Numen* (1954), pp. 186 f.; *Myth, Ritual and Kingship,* ed. S. H. Hooke (Oxford, 1958); E. O. James, *The Ancient Gods* (New York, 1960), pp. 134 ff.

[3] M. Eliade, *Images et Symboles* (Paris, 1952), p. 73: ' . . . un mythe raconte les événements qui ont eu lieu *in principio,* c'est-à-dire "aux commencements", dans un instant primordial et atemporel, dans un laps de *temps sacré.* Ce temps mythique ou sacré est qualitativement différent du temps profane, de la durée continue et irréversible dans laquelle s'insère notre existence quotidienne et désacralisée.'

character. Later within this chapter it will be shown how myth has the capacity to assimilate and refashion changes within the structure of the world order, whether they are of a religious or of a political nature. Our purpose at this point is merely to emphasize that the myth and the cult in their mutual relationship create an intelligible unity between the past and the present and between the this-worldly and the other-worldly.

The function of the cult is to actualize a world order. This is not just any order, but the *real order*. To understand this concept a brief glance at the content of myth is necessary. Not every story with a reference to a primeval event can be classified as a true myth. In order to be a myth, such a story must bear a 'truth', that is, myth must relate to the basic structure of being within the world order. This 'truth' consists in a recognition of the life-determining reality which the mythical mind has apprehended in the powers of nature. Pettazzoni has worked out this distinction in an interesting manner.[1] The primitive man distinguished between 'true' and 'false' stories. Tales are considered false when their content is 'secular', concerning itself with merely external phenomena of the world such as the adventures of the prairie wolf. In contrast to this, a story is 'true' when its content is 'holy'. Such stories concern themselves with the creative acts of power of the primeval age which establish the order of being, such as the discovery of the hunt and agriculture, or the origin of life and death.

The human mind creating the myth perceives as supreme reality the great processes within nature, such as procreation, birth, and death. The overwhelming impressions of these realities find a shape in the formation of myth. To establish the present world order the myth is projected into a timeless age of the past. Because man experienced the reality of growth and decay in his fields, this experience is expressed, for instance, in the form of the Tammuz myth, the god of growth and decay. The present world order

[1]R. Pettazzoni, 'Die Wahrheit des Mythos', *Mythe, Mensch und Umwelt* (1950); Gaster, *Numen* (1954), pp. 208 f. is correct in criticizing the ambiguity of the word 'truth' in Pettazzoni's thesis. However, he has accepted the validity of his proof for the two categories of story among the primitives.

stablished by a victory in the past does not continue automatic-lly. It must be constantly reactivated in the drama of the cult. Therefore, each year Tammuz dies in the cult, and arises again in he spring accompanied by the wild joy of the expectant partici-ants. It is obvious that no actual history in the sense of a causal equence of events is possible. What once happened in the prime-al time to determine reality repeats itself each time anew in the ult. The mythical man found in these stories about the activity of he gods the integrating factor for an understanding of reality.

B. THE MYTH IN PRIMITIVE RELIGION

There have been many excellent investigations of the myth mong primitive peoples, but generally these have been specialized nd have dealt with only one tribe. In recent years it has been the vork of A. E. Jensen[1] especially which has attempted to offer a omprehensive perspective of the field. Jensen has clearly demon-trated the relationship between the experience of reality by the rimitive man and the creative power of myth formation. He finds 1 the myth the key to an understanding of the entire religious vorld view of primitive man.

From this expedition to the East Indies, Jensen cites several xamples of the mythology of the Wemale tribe. The myth of Iulua Hainuwele (coconut palm twig) is recounted as follows:[2] n primeval times, before there were any coconut palms on the arth, there was a man called Ameta who found a pig one day hile hunting. The pig, however, drowned in the water as it ttempted to escape. Ameta fished the dead pig out of the water nd found on its tusk a coconut. That evening, as he slept, he reamed of the coconut. In his dream he received the command o plant the nut, which he did. After three days a palm had sprung p into full growth. As Ameta climbed into the palm to cut its ower for a drink, he cut his finger by accident. His blood dripped n the flower of the palm. Again after three days he saw that the

[1] A. E. Jensen, *Hainuwele* (Frankfort, 1939); *Die drei Ströme* (Leipzig, 948); *Das religiöse Weltbild einer frühen Kultur* (Stuttgart, 1948); *Mythos und ult bei Naturvölkern* (2nd ed., Wiesbaden, 1960).
[2] Jensen, *Hainuwele* (1939).

blood had joined to the juice of the flower and had formed a child. He took her and wrapped her in a leaf of the coconut palm. Following another three days the child developed into a marriageable young girl named Hainuwele.

During the time of the great Maro-Dance, Hainuwele placed herself in the centre of the dancing space where for nine evenings she divided various gifts to the dancers. On the ninth evening the men of the tribe dug a deep hole. Hainuwele was seized, thrown into the hole and murdered. On the following day Ameta found her body buried in the hole. He divided it into many parts, and with the exception of the arms, buried it. Each piece then transformed itself into things which up to that time were unknown on the earth, chief among them being the tribe's staple food, the coconut. With the arms of the girl he constructed a large gate through which he challenged all the men of the tribe to pass. Those who were unable to do so were changed into animals. In this way the animals of the earth were created.

We have related this myth in some length because it exhibits so many typical characteristics of primitive myth. In the first place, the story takes place in the primeval age, before the world had received its present order of being. The myth is concerned with the great realities through which life is determined, namely, death, fertility, and the origin of the fruit tree. The decisive moment occurs in the killing of the patron deity (*Dema-Gottheit*) with whose death the *Urzeit* (primeval time) ceases, and the present life with its birth, nurture, and death commences.

When we turn our attention to the cultic ritual of the Wemale tribe, we clearly see the importance of myth. The ceremonies of fertility are all strongly connected with this event of the primeval age. Since the origin of the coconut tree is connected with the death of Hainuwele, all fertility of life is understood only in connexion with death. The woman who is sterile slaughters a pig which is then divided and buried. Still later a cultic meal is eaten. In this cultic rite the original power of the primeval age is actualized and again set into motion. The participant experiences anew the death and resurrectionof Hainuwele evidenced in fertility.

Furthermore, every child at his birth is wrapped in a palm of the coconut as in the myth. As is often the case, a connexion was soon made with the moon. Hainuwele received the characteristics of a moon deity who, as the moon waned, died in cultic ceremony. Finally, Jensen has offered strong evidence that even the cannibalism of West Ceram belongs to the cultic repetition of the primeval event.[1] We see, therefore, that all the particulars of the cult are understood in their relation to the myth. The myth carries the punctual actualization of the primeval act in the cult and affords the continuity of the event.

Paul Wirz has presented a similar scheme in the tradition of the Marind-anim.[2] These myths are concerned again with various occurrences in the primeval time which are central in the life of the tribe. One myth derives the discovery of fire from an original sexual act of the past. In the secret cults of the tribe this is dramatically re-enacted, especially in connexion with the rites of initiation. In order to initiate their youth into the secrets of the past, a girl is killed and eaten as in the *Urzeit*. The meaning lies again in the myth. The cultic drama is not merely a ceremony of commemoration, but an actualization of the mythical past. The *Urzeit* becomes the present and re-establishes through the cult the real order of the world.

One notices among the primitives the failure of a sense of time and history. Preuss reports the following story of an old man from the tribe of Matotela in North Rhodesia, who was speaking about the time when God sent death into the world: 'Yes, it was a long time ago, so long ago that even the white man had not come to the land. It was before my father's days, even before the days of his father and both died as old men . . . It was at that time before men grew old and died'.[3] The lack of a sense of history very easily allows a confusion in time to occur and relatively recent events are seen as part of the primeval age. It is essential to the myth that

---

[1] Jensen, *Das religiöse Weltbild*, pp. 43, 56.
[2] P. Wirz, *Die Marind-anim von Holländisch-Süd-Neu-Guinea*, II (Hamburg, 1922), pp. 43 ff.
[3] K. Th. Preuss, *Der religiöse Gehalt der Mythen* (Tübingen, 1933), p. 13.

anything new in the life of the people influencing their concept of world order is assimilated in this manner.

C. THE MYTH IN SUMERIAN AND BABYLONIAN RELIGION

The Sumerian and Babylonian myths share much in common with those of the primitives. In the same manner the Babylonians were impressed from every side with the overwhelming powers of their surroundings. The experience of superior forces which could suddenly and completely shatter their whole life remained for them an unchangeable reality. Their myths turned about the relation to these dreaded realities in nature. While we can conclude that there was a common human reaction to certain impressions of nature, we nevertheless observe that the new direction of the Babylonian culture had a strong effect on the formation of their myths. Especially with the discovery of writing, the sense of chronology and time sequence was developed. We are able on the basis of the Sumerian myths to study the myths first in their earliest form, and then trace them as they developed under the influence of the Babylonian civilization.

A complete Sumerian myth of creation has not as yet been discovered, but from several references, we can receive a rather good impression of its content.[1] In the beginning was the primeval sea (Nammu). Out of itself it gave birth to the cosmic mountain, which comprised both the heaven (An) as well as the earth (Ki). This couple conceived Enlil, the god of the air. We learn more from another fragment embedded in another myth.[2] The myth begins again in the primeval time with a description of the new order of being: 'After heaven had been moved away from earth, after earth had been separated from heaven, after the name of man had been fixed. . . .' Then the disturbing element enters. Most probably, Kur, the god of the underworld, had instigated the battle by carrying off the sky-goddess, Ereshkigal. Seeking revenge, Enki in his boat attacks Kur who most probably was conceived of as a dragon. We are not instructed about the outcome of

---

[1] S. N. Kramer, *Sumerian Mythology* (Philadelphia, 1944), pp. 30 ff.
[2] *Ibid.*, pp. 37 ff.

the battle. In any case the actual beginning of the world age occurs with this event. We see here what an important role the primeval water has played and how the existence of the earth is derived from chaos. A creation is not taken for granted, but is connected with the primeval struggle for victory.

The story of 'Enlil and Ninlil'[1] is a myth which is primarily concerned with the organization of the world structure. The action takes place in Nippur and is projected back into the *Urzeit* before the creation of man. The myth relates how Enlil with the moon-god Ninlil, procreated the three deities of the underworld. Although the action is not always intelligible, in general the sense is clear.[2] The myth attempts to explain the relation between the moon and the nether world. In answer to the question: 'Why is the moon so different from the underworld if they are kin?', the myth finds the solution in the violent disposition of Enlil.

Then again in the myth of 'The Journey of Nanna to Nippur'[3] there is another attempt to understand the world order. The story reflects the period in Sumer's history about 3000 B.C. when Nippur possessed hegemony. The patron god of Ur, Nanna, comes to Nippur to seek the favour of Enlil for his city. He arrives with many gifts, makes his request, and is received graciously. 'He gave him, Enlil gave him, to Ur he went. In the river he gave him overflow, in the field he gave him much grain, in the swampland he gave him *grass* and *reeds*. . . .'[4]

For the Babylonians the growth and death of the fields played an important role also. This 'truth' is seized upon in the myth of 'Inanna's Descent to the Nether World'.[5] The myth relates how Inanna, the goddess of the heavens, journeys to the nether world in search of Tammuz. There she is captured. The characteristics of fertility rites are especially noticeable in the late form of the myth: Since Ishtar has gone down to the Land of no Return, the bull

---

[1]*Ibid.*, pp. 43 ff.
[2]Cf. T. Jacobsen, *The Intellectual Adventure of Ancient Man* (Chicago, 1948), p. 152 ff. and its review by Kramer, *JCS*, II, pp. 39 f.
[3]Kramer, *op. cit.*, pp. 47 ff.
[4]*Ibid.*, p. 49.
[5]Pritchard, *ANET*, pp. 52 ff.

springs not upon the cow, the ass impregnates not the jenny...'[1]
Very similar to this is a myth of the creation of man which stems
from the first Babylonian dynasty. This myth owes its transmission
to the fact that it was embedded in a birth incantation.[2]

If we now turn our attention to the great Babylonian creation
epic, 'Enuma Elish', we find an imposing literary unit in striking
contrast to the former collection of individual myths of a loosely
linked together series. Recent scholarship[3] dates the formation
of the epic roughly in the first Babylonian dynasty, probably
during the reign of Hammurabi. This epic is concerned not primarily with the creation myth, but in the first place with a justi-
fication of the new world order brought about by the altered
political factors. The radical transformation of this epic, which
had undoubtedly a Sumerian basis, demonstrates to what extent
the myth was capable of adjusting itself to a changed situation and
assuming a new form.

The epic begins in the primeval age with the birth of the gods
from the primeval waters. In contrast to the more primitive
Sumerian tradition, we see immediately the expression of a highly
developed speculation. The Babylonian impression of life as an
existence of uncertainty and threatened danger is reflected. With
the entrance of the god, Marduk, the real purpose of the epic is
revealed. The present world order is the result of a terrible battle.
Because Marduk has slain the monster, Tiamat, the world has
received its order out of primeval chaos. Furthermore, there is
testimony in the myth to the political unification of Babylon
through Hammurabi. Enlil's place has been assumed by Marduk,
patron god of the city of Babylon. In fear the gods approach
Marduk for help and swear allegiance to him.

> Thou, Marduk, art the most honoured of the great gods,
> Thy decree is unrivalled, thy word is Anu.
> From this day unchangeable shall be thy pronouncement.
> To raise or bring low—these shall be (in) thy hand.[4]

[1] *ANET*, p. 108; *AOT*, p. 209.
[2] A. Heidel, *The Babylonian Genesis* (Chicago, 1952), p. 66.
[3] *Ibid.*, p. 14.
[4] *ANET*, p. 66; *AOT*, p. 116.

In this manner the political success of Hammurabi, through whose victory Babylon received its place of leadership, was projected back to an event in the primeval age.

By this period in Babylonian history astrology had reached a high point in its development. It is not strange, therefore, that Marduk was elevated into the heavenly constellation following his victory. The 'table of fate' which pre-determined the path of the stars was handed over to Marduk. Moreover, it is significant as a parallel to the primitive myth that in the epic the creation of man is derived from a killing of the god Kingu in the primeval age. By means of the 'Enuma Elish' the entire world structure received its foundation in this monumental example of mythical thought.

When we test the Babylonian cult, we see that once again the myth affords the actual content of their religious life. As Marduk in the primeval age had overcome the chaos in battle, in the cult this victory is re-enacted. The yearly coronation festival[1] receives its meaning as a participation in the primeval power of this original event. The festival assures the enduring world structure for the coming year.

D. THE MYTH IN ANCIENT EGYPTIAN RELIGION[2]

Egyptian culture has been stamped in every respect by the character of the land. The burning sun in its monotonous circuit and the annual flood of the Nile with its life-giving mud were the realities which dominated its life. Because of these invariables the Egyptian conceived of his world as the centre of a static order of being. It is therefore natural that the 'truth' of this concept of life should have exercised a strong influence in the formation of the myth.

In Egypt the myth also served in the understanding of world order. As in all mythical thinking the contemporary order of being was derived from a timeless event conceived of as occurring

[1]Cf. *Myth and Ritual*, ed. S. H. Hooke, pp. 47 ff.
[2]Cf. especially S. Schott, *Mythe und Mythenbildung im alten Aegypten* Leipzig, 1945); H. Frankfort, *Kingship and the Gods* (Chicago/Cambridge, 1948).

in the past. This is the pattern we discover immediately in their creation myth:

> Many were the beings which came forth from my mouth, before heaven came into being, before earth came into being . . . before I could find a place in which I might stand.[1]

The last sentence is a reference to the first act of the sun god, the calling forth of the 'primeval hill' out of the waters of chaos. At this point the unique feature in Egyptian thought and the chief concern of the creation myth is seen: the origin of the kingdom is joined inseparably to world creation. In a text from the *Book of the Dead* there is a marginal interpretation in which this connexion finds a clear expression. 'I am Atum when I was alone in Nun (the primeval ocean). I am Re in his first appearance when he began to rule that which he had made: (gloss) What does that mean?—This . . . means that Re began to appear *as a king*, as one who existed before Shu had even lifted heaven from earth.'[2]

The Egyptian religion saw in the divine king the basic principle of world order. He mediated the power (*ka*) in order to maintain the static order of the creation (*maat*) in its primeval structure. He created the continuity between the primeval age and the present. It belonged to his highest praise that he established everything as in the primeval age.[3] The static, invariable order of being remained the norm, and the historical changes which cut across this static concept were considered unimportant. For this reason the individual personalities of the various pharaohs passed into the background while the decisive element was seen in the title: 'Son of Re'.

Not every change was dismissed as unimportant, since the experience of the rhythmic cycle of nature both in heaven and on earth carried a powerful expression of reality. It became the chief task of the myth to correlate this rhythmic change with their static concept of reality. As a timeless story of the gods the myth united the fluctuating cycle of nature with the static order of the divine

[1] *ANET*, p. 6.
[2] H. Frankfort, *Ancient Egyptian Religion* (New York, 1948), p. 52.
[3] *Ibid.*, p. 54.

ing. We see this function, for example, in the myth of Osiris and Horus.[1] This chief myth of Egyptian mythology relates how King Osiris was murdered by his brother Set. Isis, who had mourned his death, finally discovers his dismembered corpse but able to conceive from the half-animated Osiris a son named Horus. He in turn conquers Set and assumes the throne of Egypt king. On this account each reigning king is celebrated as Horus and each deceased as Osiris.

This myth was carried over into every sphere of Egyptian life. With the death of the king his power which maintained the world returned to the earth, where it continued to work for supporting the inviolable world order. Since the fertility of the land depended upon the annual increase of the Nile, the Nile became a sign of the power of Osiris. For this reason Ramses IV can address Osiris as he were the source of all life.[2] In a similar manner, the power of the dead god shows itself in the growth of the grain. Because the cow remained the symbol of fertility, the Egyptian spoke of 'Horus the Bull' and 'Hathor the Cow'. Then again, the step toward an extension of this concept to the cosmology was not difficult. In the Ennead of the theology of Heliopolis, Osiris is designated as the son of Geb and Nut, thereby linking together heaven and earth in their king. Finally, the intensive concern of the Egyptian with the life after death added much to the spread of the Osiris myth. In the myth an eternal static truth was discovered which absorbed even the irrevocable changes of death. The myth explained the rhythmic movement of the natural processes in the language of eternal 'truths'. Through the connexion with the divine king the cyclic movement was harmonized with the static world order. It is obvious that no true concept of historical writing could develop within this mythical framework.

We shall briefly summarize the results of our study of myth as phenomenon in comparative religion. Myth is a form by which the existing structure of reality is understood and maintained. It

[1]For a critical treatment: A Kees, *Totenglauben und Jenseitsvorstellungen der en Ägypter* (Leipzig, 1926).
[2]Frankfort, *Kingship and the Gods*, p. 190.

concerns itself with showing how an action of a deity, conceived of as occurring in the primeval age, determines a phase of contemporary world order. Existing world order is maintained through the actualization of the myth in the cult.[1]

[1]J. L. McKenzie, in his thorough article, 'Myth and the Old Testament' *CBQ*, 21 (1959), pp. 265–282, tends to define myth as a symbolic expression of transcendental reality which is not capable of being otherwise expressed In our opinion, those who stress the symbolic role of the myth usually fai to take seriously enough the role of the cult and its function, in conjunction with the myth, of preserving the given world order. Moreover, the symbolic interpretation does not actually come to grips with the problem of the friction aroused in the tradition because of the struggle with the myth Cf. the recent article of James Barr, 'The Meaning of "Mythology" in Relation to the Old Testament', *VT*, 9 (1959), pp. 1 ff., with whose position we are in fundamental accord.

III

MYTH IN CONFLICT
WITH OLD TESTAMENT REALITY

It will be the purpose of this chapter to show the problem which was caused within the Biblical tradition when mythical material entered. By selecting particular passages we hope to demonstrate different degrees of tension existing within the text. This variation depends on the degree to which the Biblical writers have been able to assimilate or destroy the foreign understanding of reality carried in the myth. We will use the phenomenological definition of the myth as the basis of the study.

A. GENESIS 1.1–2

> In the beginning God created the heavens and the earth. And the earth was without form and void, and darkness was upon the face of the deep, and the spirit of God was moving over the face of the waters.

The simple majesty found in these opening words of Genesis has tended to conceal their difficulty for the common reader. However, since the beginning of the Christian era careful exegetes have been perplexed regarding the manner in which verse 1 should be related to verse 2. Is the chaos conceived of as being before or after the creation? Does the chaos exist independently of God's creative activity? It is rather generally acknowledged that the suggestion of God's first creating a chaos is a logical contradiction and must be rejected.[1] Also unsatisfactory is the ancient attempt to picture the chaos as the first stage in the creation since the obvious scheme of the seven-day creation is thereby destroyed.

The problem is further complicated by a syntactical lack of clarity in the translation of verse 1. Two chief opinions are represented. The first understands verse 1 as a complete sentence: 'In

[1]This was defended by Wellhausen, *Die Composition des Hexateuchs* (3rd ed., Berlin, 1899), p. 105 and revived by C. A. Simpson, *Interpreter's Bible*, I (New York, 1952) p. 468.

the beginning God created the heavens and the earth'; while the second reads verse 1 as a temporal clause subordinated to 1.3 with verse 2 as a parenthesis: 'In the beginning of God's creating the heavens and the earth' or 'when God began to create . . . then God said . . .' This problem cannot be settled solely on the basis of grammar since both translations are free from objection.[1] One of the chief reasons advanced for the latter translation is the argument of analogy. In Gen. 2.4b, there is obviously a protasis followed by a parenthesis. Moreover, nearly all Accadian cosmogonies begin with the construction *inûmi,* later *enûma,* literally 'in the day that' or 'when'. If the second translation is preferred, there is a clear statement of a pre-existent chaos independent of God's activity. Even if the first translation were accepted, the problem raised is essentially the same. Although verse 1 asserts God's creation as the beginning, verse 2 appears to set forth a prior state of chaos unrelated to the creation. Especially in the light of the Old Testament's constant disavowal of any dualistic concept of nature, the situation seems a most perplexing one.

The problem of understanding is intensified by the very nature of the Priestly creation account. Scholars have rightly emphasized the completely different atmosphere prevailing in 1.1–2.4a in comparison with 2.4b ff. In the earlier record of the Yahwist (2.4b ff.) the naïve freshness of his witness might account for any inconsistencies. However, some four hundred years later when the Priestly tradition was fixed, exactness of expression was at a premium. Von Rad characterizes the style as follows: 'Nothing is here arbitrary. Everything is thought out, weighed and to be taken precisely'.[2] One can hardly fail to recognize the conscious

[1] The first translation (defended by Delitzsch, Wellhausen, Gunkel Procksch, Eichrodt, Zimmerli, von Rad) reads *bĕrē'šîth* as an absolute, while the second (Rashi, Dillmann, Holzinger, Skinner, Budde, H. W. Robinson Albright, Simpson) treats it as a construct, followed by a genitive clause. In regard to the first translation, one would expect the pointing *bārē'šîth,* but similar constructions to *bĕrē'šîth* used as an absolute are frequent (cf. Delitzsch, *loc. cit.*). Skinner, *Genesis* (2nd ed., Edinburgh, 1930), p. 13, objects that this construction is opposed to the essentially relative idea of the waw at the beginning of v. 2, but his point is not decisive.

[2] G. von Rad, *Das erste Buch Mose* (Göttingen, 1952), p. 36. [ET, *Genesis* (Philadelphia and London, 1961), p. 45.]

ntent of the author throughout this chapter to emphasize the omplete and effortless control of God over his creation. More-ver, the Priestly writer already had the example of Second-saiah to follow, whose picture of creation absolutely vitiates any onceivable dualism (44.6; 40.26; 45.7, etc.).

In the light of this strange situation found in the text, it seems dvisable to turn our attention to the description of the chaos in .2. Perhaps by understanding the nature of the chaos, we shall be etter equipped to return with a solution to the problem raised in .1. The description of the chaos falls into three easily discernible livisions:

Section a: 'And the earth was waste and void' (*wĕhā'āreṣ āyĕthāh thōhû wābhōhû*). The verb 'was' is somewhat surprising ince in a nominal clause it is superfluous. What we actually have s a nominal clause of circumstantial force used to specify a con-lition in its proper sphere of time: 'the earth having been chaos'.[1] he noun 'waste' (*tōhû*)[2] signifies a trackless, howling wilderness, nd it can be readily seen how this could become the symbol for mptiness. The word 'void' (*bōhû*)[3] appears only three times in the)ld Testament and only in connexion with *tōhû*. The root of the ɣord is uncertain, but the *tōhû* seems to be a many-sided *bōhû*, ɣhich would account for their use together. There is no evidence hat either expression ever possessed a personal character in the)ld Testament.

[1] J. M. P. Smith, 'The Syntax and Meaning of Gen. 1.1–3', *AJSL*, 44, p. 108 f.; cf. also K. Galling, 'Der Charakter der Chaosschilderung in Gen. , 2', *ZTK*, 47, pp. 149 ff.: 'das *hāyĕthāh* statuiert die vorzeitliche Zuständ-chkeit dessen, was später Erde war'.

[2] *Tōhû* is derived from *thh* (Ugaritic *thw*) not *tĕhôm* as suggested by Caspari, ʹohuwabohu', *MVAG*, 1917, and quoted with approval by Procksch, ʹenesis (2nd-3rd ed., Leipzig, 1924), p. 441. In Deut. 32.10 it signifies a ʹilderness, parallel to *midhbār* and *yĕšîmōn*. It is used to describe a ruined city .sa. 24.10) and is parallel to *'ayin* and *'ephes* (Isa. 40.17). It appears in a gurative sense of that which is unreal, of idols (Isa. 41.29) and worthless rguments (Isa. 29.21).

[3] Perhaps the word is to be connected with the Arabic *bhy* 'to be empty', nd matched to the form *tōhû* as often occurs in pairs of words. Some have een a possible connexion with the Phoenician Baau, the wife of the wind, ʹolpia, and the primeval mother of the world (Gunkel, Procksch). This is npossible to determine, but seems unlikely. (Cf. the discussion of L. Water-ian, *AJSL*, 43, pp. 177 f.)

ʹ.R.–C

Section b: 'And darkness was upon the face of the deep' (*wĕḥōšekh ʿal-pĕnê thĕhôm*). The darkness does not belong to God's creation, but is independent of it. It cannot be understood merely as the absence of light, but possesses a quality of its own. Throughout the Old Testament it is closely associated with death (Job 38.17; Ps. 88.13 [12]; 49.20 [19]). It remains a sphere opposed to life, a land of non-being (Job 12.25; 18.18). The *tĕhôm* signifies here the primeval waters which were also uncreated. Significantly, the word always appears without an article in the singular and is feminine in gender. Following the creation, the *tĕhôm* became the waters which surround the world (Gen. 8.2). We conclude, therefore, regarding this section that the positive matter comprising the chaos is being described. It goes beyond Section a in formulating a 'something'. It complements Section a in giving it a negative character.

Section c: 'And the spirit of God was moving over the face of the waters' (*wĕrûaḥ ʾĕlōhîm mĕraḥepheth ʿal-pĕnê hammāyim*). This is an extremely difficult passage, filled with problems, which has long aroused controversy.[1] We will start with the less abstruse words. The scene of the activity is the same as in Section b, namely 'over the face of the waters'. The word *mĕraḥepheth* no longer presents the difficulties which were once encountered.[2] The verb

---

[1] J. P. Peters, 'The Wind of God', *JBL*, 30, pp. 44 f.; Albright, *JBL*, 43, pp. 363 f.; May, 'The Creation of Light in Gen. 1.3–5,' *JBL*, 58, pp. 203–4; Galling, *op. cit.*, pp. 145 ff.; W. H. McClellan, 'The Meaning of ruah Elohim in Gen. 1.2', *Biblica*, 15, 1934, pp. 517 f. (not seen); K. Barth, *Die Kirchliche Dogmatik*, III-1 (1945), pp. 112 ff. [ET (Edinburgh, 1958), pp. 102 ff.]; Harry M. Orlinsky, 'The Plain Meaning of *Rûaḥ* in Gen. 1.2', *JQR*, 48 (1957/8), pp. 174 ff.

[2] The philological evidence is as follows: The Hebrew root of *rḥp* is uncertain. In Arabic an infrequent verb occurs, but with the meaning 'to be soft'. There is an obvious connexion with the Hebrew in the Syriac where the root signifies to 'foster', 'hover', or 'brood'. The Ugaritic offers the closest parallel. Gordon, *Ugaritic Handbook* (1947), No. 1866, gives the meaning of 'soar'. In the Old Testament, the word appears once in its qal form (Jer. 23.9), and once in the piel (Deut. 32.11) beside Gen. 1.2 which is also piel. The description in Deut. 32.11 is that of an eagle teaching her young to fly. The first verb, hiph. of *ʿûr*, 'stir up', denotes the action of the bird forcing the young out of the nest. Then follows *yĕraḥēph* describing the actual process of getting the young to take to the air. This action is a hovering, shaking, flapping, but never brooding. In Jer. 23.9 *rāḥăphû* denotes a shaking or trembling of bones from fear. Köhler renders *mĕraḥepheth* in Gen. 1.2 as 'hover trembling'.

can best be rendered by some verb as 'hover', 'flutter', or 'flap'. The frequent translation of 'brood' which lent considerable support to the 'cosmic world-egg' theory of Gunkel loses its validity since the philological evidence eliminates it as a possibility.

The real difficulty turns about the phrase 'spirit of God' (*rûaḥ 'ĕlōhîm*). The word *rûaḥ* signifies, first of all, simply breath (Ezek. 37.5–8); then again, it means wind or breeze, the movement of the air (Gen. 3.8; 8.1). When the spirit of God (either Elohim or Yahweh) is spoken of, the usual meaning is of a supernatural, divine power which breaks into human life causing actions which surpass the normal human capacity. It is a divine, mysterious force upon which all life is dependent. Saul falls into ecstasy when the *rûaḥ 'ĕlōhîm* comes upon him (I Sam. 10.10). Balaam receives the gift of prophecy from the *rûaḥ* (Num. 24.2).

The first difficulty which we encounter when we attempt to apply the usual meaning of the phrase is that syntactically Section c belongs to the chaos. The *rûaḥ*, which normally has a positive meaning and belongs most definitely to God's creative work, stands over against the creation in 1.1. If the writer had wished to introduce Section c as a new element in contrast to the condition of chaos, he would have had to use a different construction, such as *wattĕraḥēph rûaḥ*.[1] As it now stands, there is the strange anomaly of having a creative force of God judged as a negative action.

There have been a number of attempts to alleviate the difficulty. It has been suggested that Section c should be translated: 'a tempestuous wind raged over the surface of the waters'.[2] This translation is based upon the suggestion of J. M. Powis Smith[3] that in the expression *rûaḥ 'ĕlōhîm*,*'ĕlōhîm* is used as a superlative. Certainly no one doubts that a superlative sense can occasionally be given a word by connecting it with a divine name.[4] How-

[1]Galling, *op. cit.*, p. 152.
[2]*The Old Testament, An American Translation*, ed. J. M. P. Smith (Chicago, 1927). A similar translation is supported by Peters, May, Galling, and von Rad.
[3]J. M. P. Smith, 'The use of Divine Names as Superlatives', *AJSL*, 45, pp. 212 ff.
[4]A. B. Davidson, *Hebrew Syntax* (3rd ed., Edinburgh, 1902), p. 49.

ever, the question at issue is whether this is a likely interpretation of 1.2. Of the many occurrences of the phrase *rûaḥ 'ĕlōhîm*, no single instance in the rest of the Old Testament can be brought to bear where this interpretation is warranted. The attempt, therefore, to eliminate from verse 2 all positive relationship with verse 1 cannot be carried through.

Then again, Gunkel has suggested that it is impossible to bring into harmony the concept of the spirit of God in 1.2 with the creation in 1.1. He writes: 'The creative God and the brooding spirit have actually no inner relation, but are mutually exclusive. The concept behind the brooding of the spirit is that the chaos develops from within itself. The creative God, on the other hand, applies his will from outside upon the world.'[1] In our opinion, this exegesis has been coloured far too much by the false translation of the word *mĕraḥepheth* as 'brood' with the subsequent reading in of the mythological. There is nothing in the word to suggest that the spirit is attempting to effect a creation from the chaos. There is merely a relationship expressed. Moreover, it seems to me that the passage is over-interpreted when Barth, building on Gunkel's exegesis, interprets 'the spirit of *ĕlōhîm*' as distinct from the *'ĕlōhîm* in verses 1 and 3. According to his interpretation, 1.2 presents a 'caricature' of a creation vainly attempted by the 'God of this world'.[2] If the Genesis writer were attempting such a contrast, he would have had to differentiate in his use of the term *'ĕlōhîm*. Otherwise the reader could never have known that the *'ĕlōhîm* of verse 2 is the antagonist of the *'ĕlōhîm* in verses 1 and 3.

Our opinion is that one has to understand the 'spirit of *'ĕlōhîm*' as a continual action over against the chaos by the creative God of verse 1. Gen. 1.2c does not begin the creation since syntactically it is part of the chaos. It merely expresses a relationship of co-existence between 1.1 and 2 since 1.2 describes a chaotic condition existing independently of God's creative activity. Moreover, the unresolved tension between these verses is of such a nature as to suggest that we are dealing with materials foreign to Israel's

---

[1]Gunkel, *Genesis* (4th ed., 1917), p. 104.
[2]Barth, *Die Kirchliche Dogmatik*, III-1, p. 119. [ET, pp. 107 f.]

tradition. Where else in the tradition of Israel do we hear of a primeval reality existing independently of Yahweh? Let us examine this material to see if there are other signs pointing to a foreign origin.

Ever since the exhaustive analysis of Gunkel's *Schöpfung und Chaos* (1895) a connexion has been taken for granted by Old Testament scholarship[1] between *tĕhôm* and the Babylonian monster Tiamat, the female personification of the primeval waters. Philologically *tĕhôm* is the Hebrew equivalent of Tiamat. The undetermined form of the female noun *tĕhôm* points to its original usage as a proper name. Although the present usage of the word in Gen. 1.2 has little in common with Tiamat, Gunkel has shown convincingly that the Old Testament does possess traditions in which the *tĕhôm* is connected with a primeval battle which initiates the creation (cf. Isa. 51.9–10). Also a description of chaos in terms of water could hardly be indigenous to arid Palestine (cf. 2.4b ff.), but points to the climate of Babylonia. We conclude, therefore, that the material found in Gen. 1.2 has its roots ultimately in myth.

It is not enough to point out interesting parallels, no matter how striking. How is it to be explained that foreign myth found its way into the Hebrew creation account? The question must be taken seriously, especially when we recall the nature of the Priestly writing. Again, it was Gunkel[2] who brought forth arguments that the infiltration of Babylonian material occurred at the dawn of Israel's history. His arguments are too well-known to need repetition. In brief, his reasoning was based chiefly on internal evidence which pointed to a long period of struggle to assimilate this material within Israel. The most serious attack on Gunkel's thesis came from Mowinckel,[3] who, on the grounds of a new

---

[1]A. Heidel, *The Babylonian Genesis* (Chicago, 1951) presents arguments which carry little weight against Gunkel since they are dominated by a particular theological standpoint which does not do justice to the material. For example, to argue (pp. 104 f.) that because Rahab in Isa. 30.7 occurs as a designation for the Egyptian crocodile, we can assume the same meaning in Isa. 51.9, is hardly a convincing method of exegesis.

[2]Gunkel, *op. cit.*, pp. 119 f.

[3]S. Mowinckel, *The Two Sources of the Predeuteronomic Primeval History (JE) in Gen. 1–11* (Oslo, 1937); *JBL*, 58, pp. 88 ff.

source criticism, attempted to prove that the entry of the foreign material came in during the Assyrian period. In his reply to Mowinckel, Albright[1] defended Gunkel's position, but supported it chiefly with external evidence drawn from archaeology. He concluded that it is impossible for material to have entered at this date which is so closely linked with the patriarchal tradition and which shows none of the characteristic signs of Canaanite mythology prevalent from the seventh to the fifth century. He suggested,[2] rather, that the 'Amorites' and the Proto-Aramaeans brought the oral traditions to the Upper Euphrates region during the period following 2000 B.C., since by 1750 the main cities from Syria to Babylon were ruled by Amorite dynasties. These traditions were then brought from northern Mesopotamia by the Hebrew ancestors into Canaan before the middle of the second millennium. The older view that the Babylonian traditions were mediated through the Canaanite culture seems less likely following the discoveries at Ugarit.[3]

---

[1]Albright, *JBL*, 58, pp. 93 ff.

[2]Albright, *From the Stone Age to Christianity* (2nd ed., Baltimore, 1946), pp. 180 f.

[3]The discoveries at Ugarit have demonstrated the complexity of the dragon mythology. Even Gunkel, shortly after publishing his epoch-making book, had begun to realize the tradition was more varied than he had first suspected, cf. H. Schmidt, *Jona* (Göttingen, 1907), p. 89. From our fragmentary knowledge of Canaanite mythology, it is evident that the dragon fight existed in various forms. Thus the smiting of Lotan (I AB) is a different mythical tradition from the battle of Baal with Yam (III AB, A). However, in both these myths the battle is not connected with the original creation of the world. The prophets often reflect dependence on this Canaanite tradition without reference to the creation (Amos 9.3; Isa. 51.9 f.; Isa. 27.1; Nahum 1.3 ff.; Hab. 3.8). Cf. Lods, *RHPR*, 16 (1936), pp. 113 ff.; Eissfeldt, *Ras Schamra und Sanchunjaton* (Halle, 1939), pp. 144 f.; Baumgartner, *TR*, 12 (1940), p. 188; 13 (1941), p. 163. Nevertheless, the Canaanite material has been worked into the framework of the Babylonian chaos myth. Humbert, *AO*, XI, pp. 235–237 has shown that in the Old Testament all the references to the dragon fight actually have the one enemy of Yahweh in mind. The chaos myth entered Israel's tradition from Northern Mesopotamia, but as the Hebrews came in contact with the Canaanite mythology they used it to fill in this original mythical tradition. Cf. the more recent discussion in J. Gray, *The Legacy of Canaan* (Leiden, 1957), pp. 26 ff.; O. Kaiser, *Die mythische Bedeutung des Meeres in Ägypten, Ugarit und Israel* (Berlin, 1959); S. E. Loewenstamm, *IEJ*, 9 (1959), p. 260; M. Dahood, *JBL*, 80 (1961), pp. 270 f.

We have presented the argument thus far that both internal and external evidence indicate that the description of the chaos in 1.2 belongs to an original body of foreign mythical material which has entered into the tradition of Israel. We have also seen the signs of tension which resulted. It is now our concern to show that two different concepts of the reality of the world were in conflict. This resulted in a process of assimilation in which the Old Testament understanding slowly destroyed its rival. We shall try to understand the Old Testament's concept of the world as presented in Genesis 1 before we study its conflict with the myth.

The present form of Genesis 1 is significant because it is a late recension of an earlier form. It provides an interesting avenue to the Priestly understanding of the creation since, in the process of assimilation, the particular concerns of this witness become especially clear. The first of the Priestly revisions is the imposition of the pattern of *fiat* creation upon a previous scheme. The Priestly writer has reinterpreted the root '*śh* (to make) in the light of the post-exilic emphasis on God's transcendence. We see, for example, that in 1.7: 'God made the firmament and divided . . .' is preceded by 1.6: 'God said, let there be a firmament . . . and let it divide . . .' The Priestly writer did not discard verse 7 but merely reinterpreted it by the insertion of verse 6. The same reinterpretation by addition is evidenced throughout the creation account. 1.14–15 presents the creation of heaven as a *fiat* act over against 1.16–17. 1.20 interprets fish and birds as a *fiat* act of creation over against verse 21 etc. It is not our purpose to present a detailed analysis of the older account, but merely to show the tendency of the writer in assimilating older material into a new theological framework.

The second indication of reworking has been noted by Old Testament scholars for a long time. The present disposition of six days in Genesis 1 is constructed upon an earlier structure of eight days. In order to achieve the six-day framework necessitated by the establishment of the Sabbath, two creative activities were combined respectively for the third and six days. The purpose of this redaction is clear: the creation of the world has been inextricably joined with the ordering of time. The first Sabbath was established on the seventh day after the creation and the Sabbaths continue in fixed order throughout the year marking the passing of time. This thought was already implicit in the creation of the luminaries as signs (*'ōthōth*) and seasons (*mô'ădhîm*). Their function was not to provide the source of light; the light had already been created in 1.3 f. independently of the luminaries. Rather, the purpose of the sign (*'ōth*) in the creation account was to assure the progression of time within the creation. They served as witnesses to the perpetuity of the creation [1] This understanding of time, emphasized by the Priestly writer in his concept of the Sabbath, stands in striking opposition to that of the Babylonians. The luminaries served for them as one of the chief means of revelation. The fate of the world determined by the gods was mirrored in the movement of the heavens. The luminaries became omens of the events of the world, but not, as in Genesis, a marking of God's creation in time. In the cyclic thinking of astrology, time has no particular significance. It is only when a *history* is established that the marking of a progression achieves importance.

These two examples of Priestly redaction are helpful in making clear the particular theological concerns of the author as he refashioned the traditions he had received. However, the theology of the writer finds its clearest expression in Gen. 1.1. It is his unique witness to the nature of the world as a reality lying outside of God. We have seen already that this verse can be interpreted grammatically in two different ways. It can be read as an independent sentence or as a temporal clause subordinated to verse 3. While there is a choice grammatically, the theology of P excludes the latter possibility. In the first place, we have seen the effort of the Priestly writer to emphasize the absolute transcendence of God over his material. It does not seem likely, therefore, that he would have left untouched the typical beginning of the Near Eastern myth nor would he have been reconciled so easily to the fact of a pre-existent chaos. This translation would be conspicuous in

[1] C. Keller, *Das Wort Oth* (Basel, 1946), p. 127.

Genesis 1 by its very lack of friction. By choosing the alternate form and reading verse 1 as a superscription, the difficulty of the pre-existent chaos is certainly not overcome. In spite of the disharmony between the two verses, the Priestly writer has sounded his witness: 'In the beginning God created the heavens and the earth'. God is the complete and sole source of the world which, by his creation, exists as a reality outside of himself.

Secondly, this conclusion is strengthened by the content of 1.1. It is a well-known fact that the verb 'create' (*bārā'*) is used exclusively of divine creation and that the accusative of the verb is always the product and never the material. In his book Rust[1] acknowledges the uniqueness of *bārā'* for the divine creative act, but objects strongly to the attempt, for example, of Eichrodt to see here a *creatio ex nihilo*. However, does not the very uniqueness lie in the fact, that to bring forth something out of nothing is without analogy in the sphere of human existence?[2] It must be acknowledged that a *creatio ex nihilo* is never explicitly expressed in the Old Testament. Nevertheless, the omission of the accusative of material along with the simultaneous emphasis on the uniqueness of God's action could hardly be brought into a smooth harmony with the fact of a pre-existent chaos. World reality is a result of a creation, not a reshaping of existing matter. To read verse 1 as a temporal clause does not take seriously enough the struggle which is evidenced in the chapter.

Finally, the use of the word *bĕrē'šîth* has often been misunderstood[3]. Rust writes: 'the normal sense of *re'shith* is the first stage of a temporal sentence'.[4] However, this is precisely not the usage in 1.1. *Rē'šîth* is not the beginning of a series, but to be taken absolutely as the opposite of *'aḥărîth* (the end). Köhler[5] sees the issue clearly when he stresses that creation in the Old

[1]F. C. Rust, *Nature and Man in Biblical Thought* (London, 1953), pp. 33 ff.
[2]W. Foerster, *TWNT*, III, p. 1007.
[3]Cf. P. Humbert, *Interpretationes ad Vetus Testamentum Pertinentes S. Mowinckel* (Oslo, 1955), pp. 85–88, and the reply of N. H. Ridderbos, *Oudtestamentische Studien*, 12 (1958), pp. 214 ff., with which we are in accord.
[4]Rust, *op. cit.*, p. 32.
[5]L. Köhler, *Theologie des Alten Testaments* (3rd ed., Tübingen, 1953), p. 72. ET (London, 1957), p. 88.]

Testament is an eschatological concept. The God of Gen. 1.1 finds the closest parallel in the 'first and last' (*rī'šôn 'aḥărôn*) of Isa. 44.6 and 48.12.

In opposition to the Priestly understanding of world reality as the free creation of a transcendent God, Near Eastern myth provides a striking contrast. The Babylonian myth of the 'Enuma elish' provides a classical example of this pattern. There was a time before world reality had been formed in which there existed only a watery chaos. From out of this chaos the gods emanated, begotten from the union of the sweet water with the primeval sea. 'Creation' was a reforming of the pre-existent matter into the present world order. While our study has indicated that 1.2 had its roots in a similar tradition, the present status of the verse shows a tremendous change. We noticed that the word *tĕhōm* has retained its feminine undetermined form but now only as a vestige without significance. The independent life once in the word has been 'demythologized' to such an extent that without the parallels from comparative religion, its mythical origin would have passed unnoticed. In a similar manner, the *tōhû* and *bōhû* have lost all connotation of a personal character to express only a formless mass. It is evident that such a tremendous change did not come about without a long history of struggle when we compare a similar tradition of chaos in an earlier stage of demythologizing (cf. Isa. 51.9–10). We see with what tenacity the mythical forms are retained.

In spite of this evidence which indicates an assimilation of the mythical concept by the Priestly writer, we are still faced with the problem of explaining verse 2. Why was this fragment retained at all since it still remains a disturbing factor? Can we assume that the writer had not fully finished his assimilation? Or would he perhaps have completely eliminated the verse if time had permitted? We are faced with the problem of determining whether or not the Biblical writer has injected a positive witness into this reworked material. The exegesis of Gunkel,[1] followed by a host of others, that this is a mythical tradition which the author was

[1] Gunkel, *Genesis*, pp. 104 f.

unable fully to integrate into his theology, is not satisfactory. The Priestly writer was far too precise to allow a half-digested fragment a place in his creation account. Moreover, Zimmerli's emphasis[1] on the inadequacy of the language to express the exact meaning of the author, while partly true, is not an adequate explanation. Rather, the direction for a positive evaluation of 1.2 has been given by Barth[2] and von Rad.[3] This verse, for the very reason of its mythical flavour, has become a useful vehicle for witnessing to a particular aspect of the creation. Von Rad finds in the verse 'a special concern of faith'. 1.2 serves to picture through its chaos, the 'negative' side of the creation. The creation is not contrasted with a condition of nothingness, but rather with chaos. This reality is not a creation of God, nor is it a dualistic principle of evil independent of God. Nevertheless, the OT writer struggles to contrast the creation, not with a background of empty neutrality, but with an active chaos standing in opposition to the will of God. It is a reality which continues to exist and continues to threaten his creation. The chaos is a reality rejected by God. It forms no part of the creation, but exists nevertheless as a threatening possibility. Thus Jeremiah pictures a return to this chaos when God rejects his people in judgment (4.23–26).

The Priestly writer has broken the myth with this affirmation in 1.1. However, he did not fully destroy the myth. Leaving those elements within the myth which he could use, he reshaped the tradition to serve as a witness to his understanding of reality. 1.1 testifies to the absolute sovereignty of God over his creation. The resistance of verse 2 to this affirmation does not stem from the inadequacy of the witness, but from the complexity within world reality itself.

3. GENESIS 3.1–5

Now the serpent was more subtle than any other creature of the field which Yahweh God had made. And he said to the woman, 'Did God say, "You shall not eat of any tree of the garden"?' And

[1] Zimmerli, *1. Mose 1–11*, I (Zürich, 1943), pp. 35 f.
[2] Barth, *op. cit.*, p. 119; III-3 (1950), pp. 406 f.
[3] Von Rad, *op. cit.*, p. 38. (ET, p. 48.)

the woman said to the serpent, 'We may eat of the fruit of the trees of the garden; but God said, "You shall not eat of the fruit of the tree which is in the midst of the garden, neither shall you touch it, lest you die".' But the serpent said to the woman, 'You will not really die. For God knows that when you eat of it your eyes will be opened, and you will be like God, knowing good and evil.'

This passage begins with a somewhat abrupt introduction of the serpent. He is characterized as the cleverest of all the animals of the field. Even more important, the serpent is one of the animals God had made. He is not Satan, nor a demon, but, according to 3.1, simply the most subtle of God's creatures. The text does not waste a single word with a description of the setting, but comes immediately to the point. The serpent addresses the woman in conversation. Milton pictures the woman utterly amazed at the ability of the serpent to speak:

What may this mean? language of man pronounced
By tongue of brute, and human sense expressed?

However, surprise is not in the text, and represents a modern point of view. The woman shows no alarm at the speaking serpent, but accepts it as a natural thing of the garden. What is surprising is the content of the serpent's conversation. The serpent begins by apparently asking a general question of information about God's command. 'Did God say you shall not eat of any tree of the garden?' Obviously the question is a caricature of God's command. Moreover, the question is so formulated as to make a simple yes or no answer difficult. No, God did not forbid eating from all the trees, but yes, God did forbid eating from one tree. It is a question to which the answer requires an explanation, since it already conceals a half-truth. The main purpose of this cunning question is achieved as the woman is drawn into conversation on the subject chosen by the serpent. Bonhoeffer, in *Schöpfung und Fall,* calls it 'the first conversation *about* God'.[1]

The woman is quick to run to God's defence. In her zeal she even exaggerates the strictness of the command. Yet the damage

[1] München, 1933, p. 63. [ET, *Creation and Fall* (London, 1959), p. 70.]

as been done. The serpent has drawn the lines along which her
answer must follow. The diabolical nature of the first question
sought from the woman was not only a repetition of God's command, but included an evaluation of it. It raised a suspicion about
the character of God. What sort of God is this who sadistically
places man in a beautiful garden only to prohibit him from enjoy-
ing it? The woman vindicates God, but her position of faith has
thereby been destroyed. She has become now for herself the judge
of God's motives. She has another source of information beside
the statement of God. A whole new field of possibilities has been
opened up to her.

That this is not reading an undue amount into the text seems
clear from the second question. The abrupt change from indirect
subtlety to blunt contradiction makes sense only on the supposition
that the first question had found its mark. Now the serpent can
unleash a frontal attack of direct contradiction and accusation.
'You will not really die!' God only threatened you to protect
himself and keep you from something good. By eating 'you will
be like God knowing good and evil'. The phrase 'knowing good
and evil'[1] is purposely vague, but its best commentary is in its
antecedent 'be like God'. The tree contained the secret of divine
knowledge which had suddenly become a possibility for the
woman to acquire. The woman had once before evaluated God's
command. Again she is faced with a half-truth and asked to judge.
The moment of decision is effected in a most delicate manner by
the author of Genesis 3. 'It is a wonderful picture which the writer

[1]The problem of determining the exact meaning of the phrase 'knowledge of good and evil' is very complex and lies beyond the scope of this
study. Cf. Vriezen, *Onderzoek naar de paradijsvoorstelling der oude semietische
volken* (Wageningen, 1937), pp. 142 ff., for a bibliography of the various
treatments up to 1937. Also P. Humbert, *Études sur le récit du Paradis et de la
chute dans la Genèse* (Neuchâtel, 1940), pp. 82 f.; Barth, *op. cit.*, III-1, pp.
285 ff. [ET. pp. 284 ff.]; A. Kolping, *Alttestamentliche Studien Noetscher*
('50), pp. 137 f.; I. Engell, ' "Knowledge" and "life" in the creation story',
Wisdom in Israel and in the Ancient Near East, ed. Noth and Thomas (Leiden,
'55), pp. 103 ff.; Buchanan, *JBL*, 75, pp. 114 ff.; B. Reicke, 'The Knowledge
hidden in the Tree of Paradise', *JSS*, 1 (1956), pp. 193 ff.; R. Gordis, 'The
Knowledge of Good and Evil in the Old Testament and the Qumran Scrolls',
JBL, 76 (1957), pp. 123 ff.

draws in 3.6, that wordless scene in which the woman stand
musing before the tree and then the decision occurs.'[1] The evil wor
of the serpent being accomplished, he disappears from the centr
of action to return only briefly as he receives the sentence of God

Even the casual reader of this chapter must catch some glimps
of the literary ability of the Yahwist. With finely etched lines th
author draws a picture of man, faced with the ultimate problem o
his existence, wrenching himself free from his relationship o
obedience to God. Nevertheless, in spite of this well-constructe
whole, there is a disturbing element which runs throughout th
chapter. Although we are immediately instructed in verse 1 tha
the serpent is simply one of the animals of God's creation, th
behaviour of the serpent hardly matches this description. We ar
amazed at his conversation. How are we to account for this dia
bolical skill of seduction? Where did he acquire this divine wis
dom about the tree? And most of all, how can we explain his out
spoken hatred for God? What seemed to be a simple snake ha
taken on a most complicated character. Behind the figure of th
serpent shimmers another form still reflecting its former lif
A tension exists because this independent life of the origina
figure still struggles against the framework of a simple snake int
which it has been recast.

It is not surprising when the answers of Old Testamer
scholars regarding the nature of the original figure are many an
divergent. The older view which saw in the snake of Genesis 3 a
analogous monster to Tiamat of Genesis 1 has little to commen
it. While it is true that both creatures possess an anti-godly hatre
their other characteristics diverge greatly. Tiamat is a fearful mor
ster in appearance, possessing cosmological powers which she use
in open battle. The snake of Genesis 3 is cunningly deceptive wit
apparently no repulsive appearance. From this comparison it
clear that Genesis 3 stems from a different tradition from Genesis

Vriezen[2] has brought forth strong arguments to support th
view that the snake in Chapter 3 was originally conceived of as

[1]Von Rad, *op. cit.*, p. 72. [ET, p. 87.]
[2]Vriezen, *op. cit.*, pp. 177 f.

magical animal, the occult source of hidden wisdom. He points
out that the root *nhš* has the meaning 'to practise divination', and
that in several places within the Old Testament the snake is
directly joined with magic (Num. 21.9: II Kings 18.4). Vriezen is
supported by Baudissin[1] who had at an early date made it very
probable that the Israelites had taken over a snake worship from
the Canaanites similar to that of the Phoenician Esmun cult.
Moreover, this claim that the snake in the Western Semitic world
was a sacred animal, the object of worship, and not an enemy of
man is further supported by archaeological evidence of the snake
cult.[2] Vriezen finds the point of the Genesis story to be a con-
demnation of all magical knowledge as anti-godly because of its
striving for divine knowledge. In addition there is a strong polemic against snake worship (also Skinner). While many of the
traits of the snake, as propounded in this theory, are present in
Genesis 3, one misses important elements through this identification. The whole side of the snake's activity as a seducer is
strangely missing from the picture. Vriezen is aware of this lack
when he attributes these characteristics of the seducer to 'a specific
Israelite-Yahwistic creation' (p. 179).[3] Furthermore, the vicious
hatred of the serpent toward God does not find an adequate explanation in the above theory. Finally, the cult plays a minor role
in Genesis 3.

Gressmann[4] finds in the figure of the snake a dualistic concept.

[1] W. W. Baudissin, *Studien zur semitischen Religionsgeschichte*, I (Leipzig,
1876), pp. 287 f.; *Adonis und Esmun* (Leipzig, 1911), pp. 325 f.
[2] P. Toscanne, 'Études sur le serpent', *Mémoires Délégation en Perse* (1911),
p. 153 ff. (The evidence is of Susa, but significant for Palestine.) H. Vincent,
'Le baal cananéen de Beisan et sa parèdre', *RB*, 1928, pp. 512–543; W. F.
Albright, *BASOR*, 31 (1928–9), pp. 1–11; S. A. Cook, *The Religion of Ancient
Palestine in the Light of Archaeology* (1930), p. 98; K. Galling, *Bibl. Reallexicon*,
1935) under 'Schlange'. Albright, 'Astarte Plagues and Figurines from Tell
Beit Mirsim', *Mélanges René Dussaud* (1939), Part I, pp. 107–120; A.-G.
Barrois, *Manuel D'Archéologie Biblique*, II (Paris, 1953), pp. 376 f.
[3] F. Hvidberg, 'The Canaanitic Background of Gen. I–III', *VT*, 10 (1960),
p. 285–294, identifies the serpent with Zbl Baal of Canaanite mythology.
In the form of the serpent he was the life-giver and healer. Similar to
Vriezen, he attributes the seductive characteristics of the snake to prophetic
interpretation.
[4] H. Gressmann, 'Die Paradiessage', *Festgabe Harnack* (Tübingen, 1921),
p. 32 f.

He brings death but is the source of life. His trait of eating dust as well as his connexion with death leads Gressmann to see in the snake an original god of the underworld. In Genesis 3 we have a combat between Yahweh, the god of the heavens, and the snake god of the nether-world. Hehn also stresses the chthonian charac ter of the serpent.[1] The theory explains very well the hatred of the snake toward Yahweh, and the desire to win Eve to his under ground kingdom. Again, the theory is not without serious diffi culties. An integral connexion between the snake and the under world is nowhere to be found in the text. The idea that the snake eats dust is an error in observation found frequently in primitive tribes and often without any mythological significance. Gress mann's theory suffers by introducing traits taken from the general history of religion which in this case distract rather than enlighten our understanding of the original role of the snake.

In the light of the above criticisms, the explanation of Gunkel still seems the most satisfactory: 'Originally the "serpent" was an evil demon having the form of a snake who was hostile to both God and man, but who was reduced in Israel to an animal'.[2] The tension exists because of the mythical elements in the earlier form which continue to shine through. The important problem now is to examine this material to see more exactly wherein the friction lies and to discover the manner in which the Biblical writer handled myth. The Yahwist was faced with the problem of ex plaining the origin and nature of sin. God had created the world as a harmonious whole. How was the present disobedience to be understood? On the one hand, he testified immediately that evil was not created by God. He excluded once and for all the possi bility that evil and good were inherent in the reality of the world due to their presence within the divine nature. Undoubtedly, it was the Yahwist who coupled together the traditions of Chapter 2 and joined them indissolubly to Chapter 3. Chapter 2 in its present form can only be understood as the background for Chapter 3 seen as its antithesis. Wholeness versus fragmentation; trust versus

[1] J. Hehn, *Festschrift Merkle* (Düsseldorf, 1922), p. 146.
[2] Gunkel, *Genesis*, p. 15.

uspicion; faith versus unbelief! On the other hand, the writer eacted just as vigorously against allowing a cosmic dualism to be is explanation. There was no power independent of God's con-rol to whom the source of evil could be attributed. The serpent as not co-existent from the beginning with God. He was merely creature who owed his existence, as did all other life, to God. he myth of a primeval principle of evil within the world was atly rejected.

Into this area, marked off by two impassable poles, the Biblical riter set the origin of sin. Bonhoeffer describes it most plastically s the strange 'twilight' which covers the account of the Fall. here is a tension which cannot be resolved, an incomprehensi-ility which rejects all rationalization, a mystery which resists nveiling. Evil is not created by God nor is it outside God's ower; nevertheless, sin is an active power, a demonic force. It is n incomprehensible hatred toward God which revolts against his uthority. Its closest Biblical analogy is found in the 'negative' eality of the chaos. However, in Genesis 3 the 'negative reality' as left the realm of mere threat to the creation to become a de-troying actuality within the creation. To communicate the com-lex reality of evil, the Yahwist employs the language of the myth, arefully altered and held in a delicate balance. Demonic elements f a Canaanite myth were associated with the serpent who epitom-zed that which is sinister and strange among the animals. The ahwist retained the demonic character of the snake arising out f the myth, but affirmed that he was a mere creature under God's ower. The tension created in the language of this broken myth eflected, although inadequately, the incomprehensibility of a eality denied existence in the creation, yet which was active and lemonic in its effect on the creation.

The Biblical writer attempted to define the limits without ;iving the answer to the problem of the origin of sin. The most mportant part of his task was a redirecting of the initial question. 'he Yahwist formed his material to focus the point of the entire tory no longer on the origin of sin, but on the nature of sin. Sin s the conscious disobedience of man to the will of God. While holding fast to the significant role of the serpent, he succeeds in shifting the full weight of responsibility on to man in such a manner as to relegate the serpent to the periphery. The serpent raised the possibility latent within man's existence. Man bears the guilt of introducing sin into God's creation by his active, conscious attempt to free himself from the divine rule.

To summarize our conclusion regarding Chapter 3: our exegesis has indicated a friction between the mythical material and its present Biblical framework. Nevertheless, in this instance it is a calculated tension which is judged by the writer as necessary in giving a true witness to the Biblical reality which he is attempting to describe. The author is in full control of his material which he radically transforms as a testimony to man's guilt in spite of the sinister mystery surrounding the revolt against God.

C. GENESIS 6.1–4[1]

6.1, 'And it came to pass, when men (*hāʾādhām*) began to multiply on the face of the earth and daughters were born unto them . . .' This verse begins without any connexion to anything previously mentioned other than a vague reference to the distant past. Grammatically the construction is clear with the apodosis beginning in 6.2. Furthermore, the *hāʾādhām* is obviously the whole of mankind.

6.2a, 'that the sons of god(s) (*bhĕnê-haʾĕlōhîm*) saw the daughters of men that they were fair . . .' It is crucial for an understanding of this passage that we determine exactly the meaning of the term 'sons of god(s)'. The phrase occurs again in Job 1.6 and 2.1, and in its undetermined form in 38.7. Closely allied are the *bĕnê ʾēlîm* of Ps. 29.1 and 89.7 (cf. Dan. 3.25). The term *bĕnê* is used in this

[1]Beside the treatment in the various commentaries, the following literature is important: K. Budde, *Die biblische Urgeschichte* (Giessen, 1883), pp 1 ff.; O. Gruppe, *Philologus*, 47 (1889), pp. 92 ff., 328 ff.; O. Gruppe, *ZAW*, 9 (1889), pp. 135 ff.; J. Wellhausen, *Composition des Hexateuchs* (3rd ed., Berlin, 1889), pp. 307 f.; F. Schwally, *ZAW*, 18 (1898), pp. 142 ff.; J. W. Rothstein, BZAW, 34 (1920), pp. 150 ff.; H. Junker, *Biblica*, 16 (1935), pp. 209 ff. (unavailable); G. E. Closen, *Die Sünde der 'Söhne Gottes'*, *Gen. 6.1–4* (Rome 1939); E. Kraeling, *JNES*, 6 (1947), pp. 193–208; J. Fischer, *Alttestamentliche Studien Noetscher* (1950), pp. 74 ff.

passage not to indicate biological sonship, but rather membership within a guild or society (Gesenius-Kautsch, 128 v.). The *bĕnê* *'ĕlōhîm* are individuals of the class 'god', just as the *bĕnê hā'ādhām* (I Sam. 26.19) are individuals of the class 'man' and *bĕnê hannĕ-bhî'îm* (I Kings 20.35) are individuals of the class 'prophet'. It is difficult to determine whether *'ĕlōhîm* has a singular or plural meaning. On the analogy of the phrase *bĕnê'ēlîm*, which is clearly a plural, perhaps the latter meaning is to be preferred. The important thing, however, is the fact that the text speaks of a plurality of divine beings belonging to the class of god.

The attempt has often been made, trying to avoid the consequences of the above interpretation, to explain the 'sons of gods' as a special type of pious or noble people (Sethians) in contrast to the irreligious or common 'daughters of men' (Canaanites). However, the occurrence of the word 'son' as a title for Israel in relation to Yahweh cannot be brought to bear as an argument (cf. Deut. 14.1; 32.5; Hos. 2.1—EVV: 1.10). Not only are these passages part of an exalted rhetorical style differing completely from Gen.6.1–4, but also these phrases do not parallel the *bĕnê* *'ĕlōhîm*. The only exact parallel would be *bĕnê Yahweh* which is strictly avoided in the Old Testament. Finally, a decisive argument against all such 'ethical' misinterpretations, is the fact that the *'ādhām* in 6.1 indicates clearly the whole class of mankind. This word cannot suddenly assume a restricted sense in 6.2. The phrase *bĕnôth hā'ādhām* indicates, therefore, the daughters within the class of mankind, and not a particular class of men.

6.2b, ' . . . and they took from them wives of all they chose.' The emphasis is on the physical attraction excited in the 'sons of gods' by the 'daughters of men'. Because of their supernatural powers, the 'sons of gods' were able to act as they wished among the daughters of mortals.

6.3, 'But Yahweh said: My spirit shall not abide (?) (*yādhôn*) with man forever, because (?) (*bĕšaggam*) he is flesh; and his days shall be a hundred and twenty years.' This verse bristles with difficulties to such an extent that it is impossible to know if a fully satisfactory solution can ever be obtained. The verse breaks so abruptly into that which precedes it that we can be sure of the work of redaction. Up to this point, we had heard nothing about Yahweh. Suddenly, we have a judgment in the form of a 'Yahweh oracle'. The verb *yādhôn*,[1] traditionally translated 'abide', has consistently resisted explanation. From the context we can only suppose that the common rendering is fairly close to its meaning. Furthermore, the 'spirit' (*rûḥî*) is difficult. Wellhausen suggested that the *rûḥî* is the divine substance common to the gods.[2] Because this had been mixed with the human spirit, a disorder entered the creation to which Yahweh pronounces a judgment. The chief difficulty of this interpretation was already felt by Wellhausen. It does not fit well with 6.3b since logically just the shortening of man's life would not prevent the propagation of the divine substance within the race. One would expect an annihilation and hence Wellhausen eliminates 6.3b as a gloss. An alternative suggestion of Dillmann (*loc. cit.*) sees the *rûḥî* as the divine principle of life, planted in man at the creation (2.7). The point of the judgment would then be that Yahweh shortens man's life to one hundred and twenty years by withdrawing his spirit. Although this interpretation seems actually the more favourable, the difficulty remains with its lack of connexion with verses 1–2. We shall return to the problem when we consider the passage as a whole.

The next two words are equally perplexing. Who is meant with the phrase 'in man'? We have contended that *hā'ādhām* in 6.1 and 2 denotes mankind in general and it would be natural to expect this meaning to continue. Why should the judgment fall on mankind? Moreover, it is difficult to see the connexion with the next word. The spirit of Yahweh was never promised to mankind 'forever'. Only if we understand the *bā'ādhām* as the new generation pro-

[1]The LXX, Vulgate, Peshitto, and Targum of Onkelos indicate the meaning 'abide', 'remain'; Symmachus renders it as 'judge'. Both of these are etymologically doubtful. In regard to the latter, there is no evidence to suppose that the root *dyn* ever appears with a waw. The many other attempts at derivation remain hypothetical. Cf. the most recent explanation, E. A. Speiser, *JBL*, 75, pp. 126 ff.

[2]Wellhausen, *op. cit.*, p. 308.

duced by the union of the 'sons of gods' with the 'daughters of men', do we get some sense out of the phrase 'forever'! The offspring of this unnatural union claim to have received from their divine fathers that supernatural substance which affords them eternal life. The LXX points to this interpretation with the translation 'in these (*toutois*) men'.

This understanding of *bā'ādhām* seems to be confirmed by the phrase which follows: 'because he is flesh'. Modern commentators are rather generally agreed that the word *bĕšaggam* is an awkward combination of the preposition *bĕ*, the relative *'ăšer*, and the adverb *gam*. This reading only has meaning when we take *bā'ādhām* (6.3) as its antecedent denoting the new bastard generation. Then the also' (*gam*) sets these beings in contrast to the rest of mankind. Yahweh withdraws his spirit, and in rejection to their claim to divinity, judges them also, like the rest of mortal men, to be only flesh (*bāšār*). *Bāšār* denotes the temporal, corruptible, and weak, side of human nature contrasted with the life-giving force of the *rûaḥ*.

6.3 concludes with the strange clause: 'and his days shall be a hundred and twenty years'. There are a whole flood of questions which arise demanding solutions. Is this referring to mankind in general or to this new generation alone? Is this the age limit on individual life or a period of grace before the punishment? First of all, the singular suffix of *yāmāw* (his days) would indicate that its antecedent is *'ādhām* of 6.3 in contrast to the plural suffix *'āhem* used in reference to the *'ādhām* of 6.1. The clause relates primarily to the new generation. However, it would seem from the content that more are included than just these. In the preceding paragraph we learned that the new generation, in spite of its claims, was like the rest of mankind 'also flesh'. The judgment includes not only the new generation, but mankind in general. The life of flesh will only be one hundred and twenty years.

We still have to determine the exact meaning of the one hundred and twenty years. Gruppe[1] was the first to present an elaborate defence for connecting the one hundred and twenty years with the period of grace before the flood. He supported it

[1]Gruppe, *Philologus*, 47, pp. 100 ff.

from a reconstructed Phoenician myth. The substance of the myth is that three generations of humanity had provoked the gods. The final act of *hybris* was the attempt of Phaethon to fly to heaven and this initiated the flood. Gruppe tried to find a reflection of this tradition in the one hundred and twenty years, since three average generations of forty years totals one hundred and twenty. The theory suffers not only from its arbitrary reconstruction, but also from its failure to recognize the basic aetiological motif in Gen. 6.1–4. It is most questionable whether the original myth had anything to do with the flood. Moreover, if the one hundred and twenty years set the time limit before annihilation, for any degree of clarity one would expect the sentence to have read: 'his *remaining days* shall be one hundred and twenty years'.

In the light of these reasons it seems preferable to interpret the one hundred and twenty years as the age limit for the individual life of man. It can be argued, of course, that we would have expected some previous mention regarding the normal length of life if the reference to the one hundred and twenty years is to have any meaning. However, we do know from Herodotus (I, 163; III, 23) that one hundred and twenty years was considered the normal life of man. Still there are many questions which escape our knowledge. We have no way of knowing whether the one hundred and twenty years indicate that once man lived longer, but is punished with shortened life as in Hesiod's *Works and Days* (130), or whether the reference is to the normal age of man beyond which no man can go. We should be careful not to impose the Priestly system of decreasing ages arbitrarily on the Yahwist account. However, the theory of Kraeling[1] does carry some weight when it stresses that this contains a polemic against the Babylonian tradition of the antediluvian kings who lived immensely long lives. The Yahwist rejects the tradition by imposing an upper limit of one hundred and twenty years.

Finally, 6.4, 'The giants (*hannĕphīlîm*) were on the earth in those days, and also afterward when the sons of gods came in unto the daughters of men, and they bore children to them. These were the

[1]Kraeling, *op. cit.*, p. 201.

mighty men (*haggibbôrîm*) that were of old, the men of renown.'
Although the etymology of the word is not certain, the meaning
of 'giant' is assured from the context in Num. 13.33. The word
appears to have been an obsolete word even at the time of the
Yahwist who explains it with the common *gibbôrîm*. The evidence
points strongly to the fact that the phrase 'and also afterwards'
(*wĕgham 'ăḥărê-chēn*) is a later interpolation. It separates *'ăšer* from
its antecedent, and logically seems to be an afterthought on the part
of a redactor who had in mind a tradition about giants (cf. Deut.
1.28; 9.2; Josh. 15.14). Once the gloss is removed, the causal
meaning of *'ăšer* (since or because) replaces the temporal. Instead
of having a prosaic reference of archaeological interest about the
presence of giants on the earth as a contemporaneous phenomenon with the marriage of the *bĕnê 'ĕlōhîm*, the original meaning of
the verse becomes clear. 6.4 forms a causal connexion with 6.1–2.
The giants are the fruit from the union of the *bĕnê 'ĕlōhîm* with the
daughters of men.

Now that we have gone over the text in detail, it becomes
obvious why the history of its exegesis is characterized by bitter
controversy. If the preceding interpretation is correct, even in its
general conclusions, then we are amazed to discover such a
passage in the Old Testament. What has this story to do with the
Hebrew faith? The passage breathes an atmosphere which seems
certainly more compatible with the mythology of Greece than the
religion of Israel. The idea of unrestrained polygamy among the
gods, depicted as masculine, and the helplessness of mortal
women to resist their advances is a common mythical motif. The
love adventures of Apollo are well-known. That similar traditions
were prevalent in Phoenicia has long been supposed from an
obscure fragment of Philo of Byblos allegedly taken from San-
chuniathon.[1] Moreover, the archaeological discoveries of

---

[1] At the end of the theogony, following the birth of Aion and Protogonos,
there is a reference to Bamemrumos and Usoos who called themselves after
their mother 'because the women of that time commingled unhindered with
those they happened upon'. Cf. text in Clemen, *Die phönikische Religion nach
Philo von Byblos* (Leipzig, 1939), pp. 21–22; also Eissfeldt, *Ras Schamra und
Sanchunjaton* (Halle, 1939), pp. 64 f. for a discussion of this fragment.

Sumerian, Accadian, Hittite, and Ugaritic mythology, while offering no exact parallel, do present abundant evidence of the promiscuity in sexual relations of the gods, often with mortals.[1] The Canaan into which the tribes of Israel penetrated was saturated with such tales. It seems the most reasonable assumption that from this source the material entered into the Hebrew tradition.

Our exegesis has pointed out the presence of a foreign particle of pagan mythology within the Hebrew tradition. Nevertheless, our most important work lies before us in answering the many questions which still demand answers. What were the disturbing elements within the myth? How did the faith of Israel react to this intrusion? Did the Biblical writer have complete control of his material or are there signs of unassimilated fragments? Certainly the great difficulty which we had with the text points to a definite process of reworking and assimilation. The present condition of the text can only be the result of an age-long struggle which reflects the scars of battle. Perhaps we can best reach an answer to these many problems by attempting to reconstruct the various stages through which the mythical material has passed. While every reconstruction rests upon a certain degree of hypothesis, the evidence appears very strong in its support. It is evident that 6.1–4 presents only a torso of the original myth. We learn nothing about the background leading up to the love adventures nor the consequences for the 'sons of gods'. Judging from the general pattern of Near Eastern mythology, the first stage of the original Canaanite myth probably related how these young gods, the physical offspring of the older generation of deities, discovered the women of the earth one day as they looked down from their mountain. They entered into relations with them, but soon discovered that mortal women do not suit them. They grow old and ugly. It is impossible to determine with precision how many of these typical features were part of the original myth. However, it is clear that the myth was aetiological in character. It explained the

---

[1]Sumerian: *ANET*, pp. 39 f.; Accadian: *Intellectual Adventure*, pp. 152 ff.; Ugaritic: Gordon, *Ugaritic Literature* (Rome, 1949), pp. 60 f.; Hittite: *ANET*, p. 125.

esence of giants as stemming from this mixture of the divine
ith the human. Thus by projecting an aspect of world reality
to the primeval times, the myth attributed the cause for this
range phenomenon to the promiscuity of the gods.

In the second stage the myth entered Israel's tradition. We can
ppose that the first mutilation occurred when it was still in oral
ansmission. The highly mythical character of such love adven-
res was offensive to the faith of Israel, but because this old
aterial had lodged itself deeply in Israel's tradition, it took a long
riod of assimilation to render it harmless. The assimilation took
ace, first of all, by shortening and repressing the beginning and
d of the myth although maintaining its aetiological character.
ost important, however, was that the heart of the myth was
stroyed, not by eliminating the expression 'sons of gods', but
y subordinating their activity to a direct judgment of Yahweh.
his came in 6.3 as a polemic against the mythical tradition. At
is stage the verses still were in their original succession, namely
2, 4, 3. The judgment, coming at the end of 6.4, was directed
ainst the new generation since the real question at issue turned
out their claims. The judgment of Yahweh was a rejection of
e claims to immortality made by this generation. The essence of
e myth was to assert that the divine spirit of the gods could be
ansmitted on the material-physical plane. In the mythical concept
 reality, there is no qualitative distinction between the divine
d the human. The Hebrew faith denied this categorically. By
lating the *rûaḥ* solely to the control of Yahweh (*rûḥî*), Israel
nfessed that this spirit remained the unique possession of Yah-
eh which he could withdraw at any time. God and man were not
erely quantitatively different. When we reflect as to what circles
 Israel at this early period would have been responsible for such
 attack on myth, it seems most natural to think of the early
bhî'îm (prophets). Here the interest in the spirit of Yahweh was
pecially active. The difficult process of assimilation is well attested
 by the mutilated text and the ambiguity of *bā'ādhām* in 6.3.

When we come to the third stage, the material gives rather
ear evidence which points to the work of the Yahwist although

obviously the stages into which we have divided the process o
assimilation are somewhat artificial. The placing of the divin
judgment (6.3) between 6.2 and 4 goes back most probably to hi
hand. This rearrangement had the effect of breaking completel
the causal connexion between the presence of giants and the illic:
relationship of the 'sons of gods'. According to the Yahwis
giants do not originate from a mixture of divinity with mortal:
The original purpose of the aetiological myth has thereby bee
destroyed. It is important to note the place where the process o
demythologizing has taken place. The reaction came against th
attempt of the myth to establish a claim of divinity through phys
cal procreation. This claim was judged as evil and the causal cor
nexion destroyed. The highly mythical story of the 'sons of god:
and their relations with mortal women was left almost untouchec
while the false understanding of world reality which the myt
fostered was destroyed.

We have noted the difficulty in determining what the Yahwis
intended with the one hundred and twenty years. It could b
either an age limit on human life or a period of grace. One thing :
clear—that the judgment contained in the one hundred an
twenty years now falls on all mankind rather than on the bastar
generation. Regardless of what the original meaning of the on
hundred and twenty years was, in its present position as an intrc
duction to the flood, one cannot help seeing some connexion wit
a period of grace before the coming catastrophe. The story serve
as an example in 6.5 of the ungodly conditions before the flooc
Disregarding the difficulty that mankind in general is punished fc
the sins of the 'sons of gods', the Yahwist has worked this materi:
into his 'history'. It serves as a plastic illustration of the increasin
sinfulness of man before God. The magnitude of sin is seen in th
appalling fact that even the divine beings transgress the establishe
order of the creator.

Our exegesis has shown the long history of the struggle t
overcome the myth. Even in the final stage the mutilated and hal
digested particle struggles with independent life against the ro
to which it has been assigned within the Hebrew tradition. In spii

f its mythical flavour, which it has retained, its new framework
idicates its role within the Biblical history. It has become a
iegative illustration', picturing that which has been rejected and
ondemned. The heart of the myth has been destroyed, but its
esisting and struggling life has been re-employed by the Yahwist
) demonstrate the opposition to God. The many unanswered
uestions and the inconsistencies[1] within the text make the
mitations evident in using such material. This is not a highly
olished segment with a calculated tension as in Chapter 3; never-
1eless, the material has been demythologized to the extent that
serves a useful purpose for the biblical writer.

). EXODUS 4.24–26

And it came to pass at a lodging place on the way Yahweh met
him and sought to kill him. Then Zipporah took a flint and cut off
her son's foreskin and touched Moses' feet with it, and said, 'Surely
you are a bridegroom of blood to me!' So he let him alone. Then it
was that she said, 'You are a bridegroom of blood', because of the
circumcision.

There are few passages within the Old Testament which have
alled forth more controversy than the account of the circumcision
f Moses' son by Zipporah. The difficulties are immediately
vident. In the first place, Yahweh, who had just commissioned
Ioses with a blessing (4.19) to free his people from Egyptian
ondage, suddenly attacks him with the purpose of killing him.
'he force of the verb cannot be reduced by suggesting a type of
unishment. Secondly, the reader has trouble understanding how
ie circumcision of the son relates to Moses' plight. Finally, the
ieaning of the enigmatic pronouncement is most obscure:
surely you are a bridegroom of blood to me!' Why should Moses
rho already has a son (cf. 4.20!) be called a bridegroom?

The traditional interpretation (Calvin, Keil, Buber, etc.) sought
) clarify these difficulties by postulating that Moses, under the
ifluence of the Midianite, Zipporah, had failed to circumcise his

[1]There are many attempts of the later Jewish writers to fill in the gaps.
f. Gressmann-Bousset, *Die Religion des Judentums* (Tübingen, 1926), pp.
32 ff.; A. Lods, 'La chute des anges', *RHPR*, 7 (1927), pp. 295 ff.; B. J.
amberger, *Fallen Angels* (Philadelphia, 1952), pp. 15 ff.

son and thereby incurred the wrath of God. Then Zipporah, realizing the cause, circumcised the son and in resentful anger against her husband hurled the foreskin at his feet with the accusation: 'You are a blood-bridegroom'. By this she meant that she had had to 'purchase him anew as a husband with the blood of her son'[1] (cf. LXX). The inadequacy of this interpretation has been felt by most modern commentators. In the first place, the discrepancy between God's commission and this sudden, sinister attack has not been clarified. One can hardly attribute this behaviour to the same God. There is nothing whatever in the text which allows the exegete to postulate that Moses had disobeyed God, nor is it legitimate to suggest that the cause lay in Zipporah's opposition to a Hebrew rite. One cannot raise the ethical level of this passage up to that of the preceding with psychological devices. Secondly, although the verb *tagga'* (4.25) can at times be translated 'throw', the meaning is unnatural to this passage. Why should Zipporah blame Moses and reproach him at the very moment his life was still endangered? The more obvious translation of the phrase is 'made to touch his feet'. The touching has a causal relation to the freeing of Moses and is not a rebuke. The traditional interpretation has completely missed the point of Zipporah's remark. Finally, the explanation of the term 'bridegroom of blood' is most artificial and unconvincing. It has failed to consider the underlying aetiological motif connecting circumcision with marriage.

Let us start our exegesis at this last point. Scholars have long recognized that this very ancient story should be classified as an aetiology. The repetition of the key phrase in a temporal clause introduced by *'āz* (then) is an unmistakable sign. The story seeks to explain a certain relationship between the term 'bridegroom of blood' and infant circumcision. As Moses was returning to Egypt from Midian he was forced to spend a night *en route*. At a certain overnight spot, presumably at night, he was attacked. The closest parallel appears in Gen. 32.22 ff. where Jacob is also attacked at night by a superhuman enemy. It is important for the story to

---

[1] S. Glassius, quoted with approval by Keil, *The Pentateuch*, I (Edinburgh 1865), p. 460.

te that it was Zipporah, daughter of the Midianite priest, who
mediately reacted with unabashed resourcefulness. Her action is
mmarized in one verse. She took a flint and circumcised her son.
ne stone implement is significant as an indication of the age of
 story (cf. Josh. 5.2). Next she touched Moses' *raghlâw* saying:
urely you are a bridegroom of blood to me'. The word *reghel* has
 meaning of foot or leg. It is easy to see how the word could be
ed euphemistically for one's nakedness.[1] With this translation
 purpose of her circumcision becomes clear. She has circum-
ed her son *instead* of her husband, and with this action has
nsferred its benefits to him. This explanation is borne out in
 phrase 'bridegroom of blood' (*ḥāthan dāmîm*).[2] The word
ḥān, meaning 'son-in-law' or 'bridegroom', is closely related to
 Arabic root *ḥathana* which means both 'marry' and 'circum-
e'.[3] The original purpose of circumcision as a puberty rite is
arly indicated. The *ḥāthān* is the circumcised one who is enter-
; by marriage into a new family relation. When Zipporah
uched Moses' nakedness, she made him symbolically a bride-
oom, i.e. a circumcised one. She thereby delivered him from the
ack of God which had been incurred because Moses had never
en circumcised.

Reviewing the story in its entirety, we see that the aetiology
ks to explain why in Israel infant circumcision had replaced the
mmon puberty rite of adult circumcision. There are many
lications that the story was only secondarily adopted into the
dition of Moses. The story has no integral connexion with
at precedes or follows, but stands rather isolated in the con-
t.[4] Moreover, the story breathes an atmosphere which is quite

---

[1] Cf. Isa. 7.20; Isa. 36.12 (Qerē); perhaps Isa. 6.2.
[2] Cf. J. Hehn, 'Der Blutbräutigam', *ZAW,* 50 (1932), pp. 3 ff. Hehn's
noval of the term can hardly be called a solution.
[3] A different etymology, cognate with the Accadian *ḥatānu* (protect), is sug-
ted by Y. Blau, 'The *Ḥatan Damim* (Ex. 4.24–26)', *Tarbiz,* 26 (1956), pp. 1 ff.
The story has been worked secondarily into the J source. In spite of the
ections of Gressmann, *Mose und seine Zeit* (Göttingen, 1913), p. 57, based
his reconstruction, most commentators see the following sequence:2.23a;
9, 20a; 4.24–26. Cf. Eissfeldt, *Hexateuch-Synopse* (Leipzig, 1922), pp. 31 f.;
th, *Überlieferungsgeschichte des Pentateuch* (Stuttgart, 1948), p. 221; somewhat
erently, Simpson, *The Early Traditions of Israel* (Oxford, 1948), pp. 431 f.

foreign to the faith of Israel. Although the God of the covena
appears often as a God of wrath, he does not act in the Old Test
ment as a sinister demon of the night who ambushes men. T
story is not concerned with the religious problem regardi
obedience and disobedience. Rather, it moves on the level
magical acts. Zipporah performs the rite, pronounces the corre
formula, and *ex opere operato* the desired effect is achieved. T
point of the story is to disclose the startling fact that infant c
cumcision 'works' in the place of adult. The friction produced
this story again indicates the entrance of a foreign tradition whi
was only secondarily assimilated within Israel. Originally, t
deity was a local night demon who by chance inhabited the par
cular place chosen by a wayfaring couple for their overnight re
He attacked the man because he was not circumcised, but w
then appeased by the quick wit of the wife who performed
vicarious operation on her son.

Eduard Meyer, followed by a great number of modern ex
getes,[1] has attempted to reconstruct from this aetiology
original story far more mythical than we have indicated. Accor
ing to this reconstruction the story was originally concerned wi
a local *numen,* who claimed on the wedding night of a couple t
ius primae noctis. Recognizing the peril, the woman circumcis
her husband, touched then the nakedness of the demon with t
foreskin and cried, 'You are my blood-bridegroom'. In this for
the story was a cult aetiology explaining the origin of adult c
cumcision as a sacrifice to the deity and protection for the bri
groom. The inner coherence and force of Meyer's hypothesis
felt immediately by anyone acquainted with the material of co
parative religion. In such a study as this, one is tempted to see
excellent example of the extent to which mythical material h
been assimilated within Israel. At this point, however, caution
advisable for sound exegesis lest one be deceived into thinki
that here is a device for unlocking all doors. While the possibil

[1] Ed. Meyer, *Die Israeliten und ihre Nachbarstämme* (Halle, 1906), p.
H. Gressmann, *op. cit.,* p. 56 ff.; Beer, *Exodus* (Tübingen, 1939), pp. 38
R. Meyer, *TWNT,* VI, p. 75.

f such an original myth is acknowledged, it does not seem prob-
ble. In the first place, the pattern of the reconstruction, while
tting together amazingly well, is taken completely from the
nalogy of comparative religion. Moreover, this involves the
erious emendation in the text of verse 25 to read 'her husband'
îšāh) in the place of 'her son' (*běnāh*).[1] Finally, and most impor-
ant, the story as it now stands is completely coherent and does
ot exhibit those vestiges which would compel the exegete to
earch for another account.

What can we now say regarding the manner by which this
naterial has been assimilated into Israel's tradition? The many
ttempts to harmonize this material smoothly into the book of
ixodus have not proved successful. Vischer's[2] interpretation
f the story as establishing a close connexion between the
.brahamitic and Mosiac covenants is not convincing since Exodus
.24–26 had found a settled place within the Yahwist source long
efore circumcision had become the sign of the Abrahamitic
ovenant (Gen. 17:P). Then again, Rudolf Meyer[3] has recently
uggested that in its present form the phrase 'you are a blood-
ridegroom to me' reflects a more developed understanding of
;od and circumcision than in its first stage. However, he has not
resented any convincing evidence to support this statement. The
resent form of the story only indicates such a development when
ne postulates as a first stage the reconstructed form of the myth
/hich we have rejected.

We suggest that the key to an understanding of the process of
ssimilation lies in discovering the basic issue of conflict between
he myth and the Old Testament witness. This fact would give us
n understanding of the struggle which has taken place. It seems
lear that the primary issue at stake was regarding the nature and
rigin of the rite of infant circumcision. The myth derived the
rigin of the rite from an event which, if not timeless, at least lay
utside the *Heilsgeschichte* of Israel. The origin of this rite was also

[1]Gressmann, *op. cit.*, p. 56.
[2]W. Vischer, *Das Christuszeugnis des Alten Testaments*, I (1935), pp. 210 f.,
T (London, 1949), pp. 170 f.
[3]R. Meyer, *op. cit.*, p. 75.

of great importance for the religion of Israel, but the problem was how to relate this rite inherited from the past to the covenant of Yahweh. The attempted solution in Exodus 4 is of great value in clarifying the manner by which the Hebrew tradition developed. It indicates a method of handling tradition which is obviously strange to the historical sense of our Western mentality, but which is central to our study. The myth was undoubtedly embedded in the folk tradition of the people. They inherited the rite of circumcision as well as its mythical explanation. However, instead of destroying the myth or substituting another explanation, the myth was retained but anchored to the *Heilsgeschichte* of Israel. That the myth was 'historicized' as an event in the life of Moses is not strange since Moses was the dominant figure of the wilderness period, from which period the myth also stemmed. By transforming the myth into a saga the basic understanding of this aspect of world reality was altered. The saga in Exodus 4 testifies that a rite as important for Israel as circumcision had its roots in God's action in Israel's history.

This leads to the second chief indication of assimilation. Although the demonic nature of the deity has been retained, it has become subsumed under the activity of Yahweh. Rather than acknowledge forces independent of his power, Yahweh himself has taken on the characteristics of a demon.[1] The result is that a tension is certainly produced. It is somewhat different, however, from Genesis 3 where the tension is between Yahweh and a mythical antagonist. In Exodus 4 there is no internal friction within the segment which has been completely assigned to Yahweh, but rather there is the friction with the main Hebrew tradition into which it has been placed.

The use of myth in Exodus 4 has a different function from the passages previously discussed in Genesis. In Exodus 4 there is no effort made to retain the mythical flavour in producing a calculated tension. Myth entered from a foreign source into Israel and embedded itself into the tradition. It provided an explanation for some recognized aspect of world reality. We find a similar situa-

[1] Volz, *Das Dämonische in Jahwe* (Tübingen, 1924), p. 31.

64

ion in Gen. 18.1 ff.; 28.10–22, and Judg. 11.34 ff., where ancient myths originating around sacred places have been historicized into the tradition of Israel. The slow process of assimilation in Exodus 4 began by transforming the myth into a saga. However, the demythologizing has not gone far enough to eliminate the friction caused by assigning demonic characteristics to the covenant God.

2. ISAIAH 11.6–9[1]

. And the wolf shall dwell with the lamb, and the leopard shall lie down with the kid,
  And the calf and the lion (shall fatten) together, and a little child shall lead them.

. And the cow and the bear (shall become friends), their young shall lie down together;
  And the lion shall eat straw like the ox,

. And the suckling child shall play over the hole of the asp.
  And the weaned child shall put his hand on the adder's (den).

. They shall not hurt or destroy in all my holy mountain,
  For the earth shall be full of the knowledge of Yahweh as the waters cover the sea.

While we are concerned for our study only with verses 6–9, the unit is obviously 1–9. Verses 6–9 are to be understood in connexion with the coming ruler who is to establish the new order for the future age. When 11.1–5, 9 are compared with 6–8, it is evident that the first verses reflect the characteristic theology of Isaiah. Such indicative words as *ṣedheq*, *'ĕmûnah*, and *rûaḥ* show his creative work clearly. However, when we come to 11.6–8, we are in another atmosphere. All characteristic marks of Isaianic style fail. Instead we have an ancient tradition of paradisal peace pictured in terms of complete harmony among the animals.

[1]Text critical notes on Isa. 11.6–9: v. 6 for *ûmĕrî'* read *yimrĕ'û* (Köhler), cf. LXX; v. 7 for *tir'ênāh* read *tithrā'ênāh* (BH, Duhm, Gray, Procksch, Köhler); v. 8 Köhler attempts to save the MT by deriving *mĕ'ûrāh* from the Accadian *mûru* (loc. cit.). The connexion, however, is doubtful since the Accadian root is *mr'* (Baumgartner, orally). The parallelism of the passage (= *ḥur*) would suggest rather the emendation *mĕ'ārath* (BH).

Gressmann especially[1] demonstrated convincingly the mythic:
background of this passage along with the related passages of Ho:
2.20 (EVV: 18) and Ezek. 34.25 ff. It did not take much searchin
in the history of religion to find many parallels of paradisal peac
in mythology.[2] The Greek tradition of such a peace found it
classical expression in Vergil's Fourth Eclogue:

> Heavy with milk the goats come home themselves,
> No more do the cattle fear the lion . . .
> Disappear will the snake, and the poison-bearing herbs.

Similarly, a golden age of peace and abundance without fear :
described in Indian mythology.[3] The closest parallel to Isaiah 1
appears in the mythical description of the paradisal nature c
Dilmun in early Mesopotamian mythology:

> The lion kills not,
> The wolf snatches not the lamb,
> Unknown is the kid-devouring *wild* dog. . . .[4]

It should not appear too strange that Isaiah employs a mythic:
tradition when we call to memory how frequently in the propheti
proclamation of the future, redemptive mythical motifs of paradis
appear. Amos pictures the latter days as possessing such a fertilit
of soil that sowing and reaping occur almost simultaneousl
(Amos 9.13 ff.). Isaiah speaks of the wilderness becoming a frui
ful field and the fruit trees being in such numbers as to constitut
a forest (32.15). Joel, in a passage closely resembling the rivers c
honey and melted butter of Persian mythology, describes 'th
mountains dripping with sweet wine and the hills flowing wit
milk' (4.18—EVV: 3.18). The trees in Ezekiel's future paradise a:
miraculous trees which never drop their leaves but bear new fru:
monthly (47.12). Finally, the future Jerusalem of Zechariah 1
possesses continuous day with all cold and frost abolished.

The most significant thing, however, in the passage of Isaiah 1

---

[1]Gressmann, *Ursprung der israelitisch-jüdischen Eschatologie* (1905), pp. 193 ff.
Der Messias (1929), pp. 151 ff.
[2]*ERE*, II, p. 680 ff.; *RGG*, IV, pp. 947 f.
[3]*Rāmāyana* IV. 43 and *Mahābhārata* VI. 7.
[4]*ANET*, p. 38.

the complete lack of tension between the mythical material and
the Isaianic. Verses 6–8 indicate no sign of internal life which
resists the new framework into which it has been worked. The
mythical material has become merely a poetic description of the
complete harmony and peace which is to prevail with the coming
of the messianic age. The animal peace is a sign that the earth is
full of the knowledge of Yahweh (verse 9). This same observation
regarding lack of tension in the use of the mythical motif of paradise holds true for the other prophetic passages which have been
cited. The mythical language serves as a colourful and moving
description of the coming world transformation.

When we begin to analyse the nature of this mythical material,
it becomes evident very shortly why the tension fails. We have
seen that the myth is a form by which man attempted to understand the world about him. With previous texts we have pointed
out the tension which arose when the mythical understanding of
reality opposed the Biblical understanding. Now the lack of tension
in Isaiah 11 is due to the fact that verses 6–8 cannot actually be
called a myth. What we have is really only a fanciful description
having its original setting within myth. The material in its present
state has lost its purpose within myth and assumed a new role.
Whereas it was once closely tied to the mythical understanding
of reality, now by losing this mythical connexion it has become a
fanciful description of a world transcending that of the senses.

This change in role can be best illustrated by pointing to
similar material which still retains its original function within
myth. In the 'Baal and Anat Cycle' of the Ras Shamra texts there
is the familiar mythical motif of the death and resuscitation of
Baal, the god of fertility. When Baal goes to the underworld and
is killed by Mot, the earth mourns. When Baal returns to life, the
earth responds with paradisal abundance. 'The heavens rain oil,
the wadies run with honey'.[1] The Ras Shamra passage arises out
of the attempt of the myth to explain and maintain the fertility of
the earth in its seasonal fluctuation. It has a part in the mythical un-

[1] A III 6 f.; Gordon, *Ugaritic Handbook*, 49, III, p. 138; Gordon, *Ugaritic Literature*, p. 46.

derstanding of reality. Although the parallels between many of t]
Old Testament passages and this description of mythical abundan·
are evident, in the Old Testament the connexion with the myth ·
the dying and rising Baal has been lost. The fragments, therefore, ¤
longer contain in themselves a mythical understanding of realit]

Then again, the Dilmun myth[1] of Sumerian mytholog
illustrates the original function of the paradise motif within t]
myth. In spite of the obscurity surrounding this myth,[2] certa·
observations can be made which touch upon our subject. T]
purpose of the myth concerns itself with the strange attraction ar
antagonism between Mother Earth, Ninhursaga, and the lif
giving water, Enki. The myth tries to establish a causal connexic
between many disparate phenomena of nature due to the fick
nature of Enki. The myth is offering an explanation of wor
order, but it sets this against the background of the world befo·
it had received its structure. Dilmun is the land pictured in t]
negative terms of existent order. 'In Dilmun the raven utters ¤
cries . . ., the lions kill not, . . . the sick-headed says not
am sick-headed" . . .' The paradise motif has its role within t]
myth as the setting from which the present world order was to]
formed in the struggle of the gods.

Let us return now to the Biblical usage of the paradise mot
We have been arguing that the lack of friction in the prophetic u
of the paradise motif is due to the loss of its essentially mythic
character. In its demythologized form its original function w·
severed, but it remained a plastic and vivid description of a wor
unknown to human experience. The prophets found in this d·
mythologized form useful material in which to clothe their esch·
tological hope. In Isaiah 11 this usage of mythical fragments b·
comes apparent. The prophet is speaking of a new age which is ·
be ushered in with the appearing of a kingly ruler on whom t]
spirit of God rests. He shall exercise impartial judgment a·
establish equity and justice on the earth. Then in an effort to d·

[1]*ANET*, pp. 38 ff.
[2]I am especially indebted to the interpretation of T. Jacobsen,]
Intellectual Adventure of Ancient Man (1946), pp. 157 ff.

scribe in a more moving manner the complete and radical transformation of the world to come, Isaiah reaches into the realm of
myth. He found in the demythologized fragments of the paradise
myth a medium which lent itself admirably to his purpose. The
qualitative difference of the new age which was to transcend
human experience was expressed in the mythical description of
paradise. There was no friction aroused because these fragments
lent themselves completely to the purpose of the prophet in describing the new reality. The words became for the prophet a
convenient and adequate symbolism by which to communicate to
Israel the nature of a new reality which God was forming in her
history.

F. ISAIAH 14.12–21[1]

12. How are you fallen from heaven, Helel, son of Dawn!
    (How) are you cut down to the ground, you who laid the nations
    low!
13. You said in your heart, 'I will ascend to heaven,
    Above the stars of God I will set my throne on high;
    I will sit on the mount of assembly in the far north;
14. I will ascend above the heights of the clouds, I will make myself
    like the Most High.'
15. Yet you are brought down to Sheol, to the depths of the Pit.
16. Those who see you will stare at you, and ponder over you:
    'Is this the man who made the earth tremble, who shook king-
    doms,
17. Who made the world like a desert, and overthrew (its) cities,
    Who did not (let) his prisoners go home?'
18. All the kings of the nations, all of them lie in glory each in his
    own house.
19. But you are cast out, away from your sepulchre like a loathed
    (vulture).
    Clothed with the slain ( ) like a dead body trodden under foot.

[1]Text criticism of Isa. 14.12–21: v. 12 retain the MT's reading of *hêlēl* with
P. Grelot, *VT*, 6 (1956), pp. 303 f. instead of emending it to *hêlāl* with the
LXX, Vulgate, Duhm, Jahnow, etc.; 12b insert *'êkh* before *nighda'tā, metri
causa* (Duhm, Marti, Gunkel, *BH*); v. 17 for *wě'ārāw* read *wě'ārêhā*; for *phāthaḥ*
read *phittaḥ* or *phittēaḥ*; v. 17b both text and metre are uncertain. LXX omits
bayěthāh. However, the major emendations adopted by Budde, Marti, Jahnow,
Procksch to correct the *hysteron proteron* do not seem justified; v. 19 for *kěněṣer*
read *kěněṣer* (Köhler); move *yôrědhê 'el-'abhnê-bhôr* to the beginning of v. 20
(*BH*). Jahnow holds it to be a gloss. The change in metre indicates a probable
corruption; v. 21 omit *'ārîm* as a gloss, *metri causa* (Duhm, Gunkel, etc.).

20. (Like those who go down to the stones of the Pit), you will not
    be joined with them in burial.
    Because you have destroyed your land, you have slain your people.
    May the descendants of evildoers nevermore be named!
21. Prepare slaughter for his sons because of the guilt of their fathers,
    Lest they rise and possess the earth, and fill the face of the world ( )

This passage is a taunt song concerning the fall of the king of
Babylon written in an imitated style of a funeral song. As early in
the history of exegesis as Herder this song has been recognized as
a myth. The key to the interpretation is found in the name *hêlē
ben-šaḥar*.[1] The earlier exegetes wanted to connect the word with
the Arabic *hilāl* meaning 'new moon', but it was Gunkel once
again who recognized Helel as the morning star.[2] This interpretation was, however, actually found already in the old versions
(LXX, *heōsphoros*; Vulgate, *Lucifer*).

Verse 13 informs us that Helel attempted to ascend to the
heavens, to sit on the 'mount of assembly in the far north' (*běhar
mô'ēdh běyarkěthê ṣaphôn*), to be like the Most High (*lě'elyôn*). The
name Baal Zaphon indicates immediately that we are in the realm
of Canaanite mythology. Eissfeldt[3] has advanced good reasons
why *běyarkěthê ṣaphôn* should be translated 'on the top of Zaphon'.
Especially in the light of the parallel construction in verse 15
yarkěthê bhôr (the depths of the pit) is very probably a place name.
Mount Zaphon, as the seat of the deity, is then the place of
assembly for councils among the gods. The name of this highest
god is *'elyôn*. On the basis of archaeological evidence there can no
longer be any doubt that we have here a Canaanite deity, the chief
god of the pantheon.[4]

---

[1]Köhler has demonstrated that *šaḥar* denotes that brief moment before
the break of dawn, translated as closely as possible by the German 'Morgen-
röte', *ZAW*, 44 (1926), pp. 56 ff.

[2]Gunkel, *Schöpfung und Chaos*, pp. 132 ff.

[3]Eissfeldt, *Baal Zaphon, Zeus Kasios, und der Durchzug der Israeliten durch
Meer* (1932), pp. 14 f.

[4]On the basis of a stele found in Sefire, south-east of Aleppo in 1930
Hempel concludes (*ZAW*, 50 (1932), p. 182): ' . . . der 'Aeljon, der damit
endgültig als selbständiges altsyrischer Gott erwiesen ist'. It is especially the
Ras Shamra texts which gives us a real insight into the nature of this god. Cf
Bauer, *ZAW*, 51 (1933), pp. 96 f. Compare also the discussion of Dussaud,
Les Religions des Hittites et des Hourrites, des Phéniciens et des Syriens (Paris, 1945,
pp. 359 ff.

With this evidence we shall try to reconstruct the myth. As Gunkel rightly saw, we are dealing here with a nature myth. The mythical mind saw a cosmic battle between Helel and Elyon in the brilliant rise of the morning star in the heavens with its sudden dimming before the increasing rays of the sun.

The myth was placed within the familiar framework of the rebellion of the younger god against the ruling head of the pancheon.[1] Insolent Helel wished to challenge the power of Elyon. His successful beginning was soon thwarted and he was thrown down to the pit of Sheol. The prophetic writer has taken this old myth and reworked it into his taunt song. He compares the mighty king of Babylon to the upstart, Helel. He also had a brilliant start, but then Yahweh hurled him down to become the laughing stock of the nations.

In the light of the above linguistic evidence there can be little doubt that this myth had its origin in Canaan. The suggested parallels from Babylonian literature, for example, the Etana myth,[2] have only a vague connexion. However, an exact parallel in Canaanite literature has not yet been found.[3] The figure of Shahar appears in the literature of Ugarit as the son of El and twin brother of Shalem,[4] but in another context. Albright suggests that Isa. 14.13 may perhaps be an actual quotation from a Phoenician (Canaanite) epic in view of the similarity in style to the Canaanite epic of Aliyn Baal and Mot.[5]

The significant factor for our study is that, in spite of the highly mythical nature of the material, the framework into which it is now placed has had the effect of thoroughly demythologizing it.[6]

---

[1]Cf. Morgenstern, *HUCA*, 14 (1939), pp. 109 ff.; M. Pope, *El in the Ugaritic Texts* (Leiden, 1955), pp. 27 ff.

[2]*ANET*, pp. 114; *AOT*, pp. 235 ff.

[3]Cf. the rich comparative material offered by P. Grelot, *RHR,* 149 (1956), pp. 18–48.

[4]Gordon, *Ugaritic Literature*, pp. 60 f. Cf. Gaster, 'A Canaanite Ritual Drama', *JAOS*, 66 (1946), pp. 69 ff.; G. R. Driver, *Canaanite Myths and Legends* (Edinburgh, 1956), pp. 22 f.

[5]Albright, 'The North Canaanite Epic of Al'eyan Ba'al and Mot', *JPOS*, XII (1932), p. 192, note 22.

[6]Cf. G. Quell, 'Jesaja 14,1–23', *Festschrift F. Baumgärtel* (Erlangen, 1959), pp. 131–157, for a recent analysis of the framework.

The myth of Helel has become merely a striking illustration dramatizing the splendour of the rise to fame and the shame of the fall which is sarcastically hurled at the king of Babylon. There is no tension whatever between the myth and its Old Testament framework since the myth carries only illustrative value as an extended figure of speech. It was a serious misunderstanding of this passage when Christian commentators (Tertullian, Gregory the Great, etc.) interpreted the fall of Helel in the light of Luke 10.18 as referring to the pre-history of Satan and revived a mythology already overcome in the Old Testament.

We should like to summarize the results of this chapter. The exegesis has shown varying degrees of conflict at the point where mythical material entered the tradition of Israel. This conflict was caused by the intrusion of an understanding of world reality which opposed the Biblical. By reconstructing the history of the struggle in several instances the manner by which the Old Testament assimilated the mythical material has been demonstrated. The study has also shown that the assimilation process was effected only gradually and in varying degrees. At times the Biblical writer was completely able to control his material, while at other times the resistance inherent within the myth has continued to struggle against its new framework. Finally, the study has shown that the Old Testament made use of the broken myth in performing a service within its own witness. However, the role of the broken myth within the Old Testament is not uniform. At times the mythical vestiges have been left in a passage to obtain a calculated tension. The myth served to illustrate the active opposition to God's purpose. Also the myth served in a historicized form as a saga within the Old Testament *Heilsgeschichte*. Finally, an important role was played by virtue of its imaginative language. Examples were found in which the broken myth served merely as an extended figure of speech. Far more significant, however, was the role played by the broken myth in picturing the reality of the eschatological age.

IV

THE OLD TESTAMENT'S CATEGORIES
OF REALITY

Our study of selected texts has pointed out the conflict which
arose when the Old Testament's concept of reality came into conflict with myth. Up to this point we have approached the Old
Testament's understanding of reality from the point of view of its
negative reaction to the myth. We now turn to analyse in a more
positive fashion its concepts of reality as expressed in the categories of time and space. The unique elements of Biblical thinking
can best be seen by contrasting them with mythical thinking. In
using the term mythical thinking we intend to turn our attention
away from the individual myth to the thought patterns underlying myth in general.

A. THE CONCEPT OF TIME

1. *An Analysis of Mythical Time*[1]

The concept of time found in the myth is, first of all, characterized
by its understanding of time as absolute. Time stems ultimately
from the one primeval act of power before which there was no
time and beyond which one cannot pass. This dividing line which
separates the world of being from that of non-being marks off the

[1]The following treatments were the most helpful: H. Hubert and M.
Mauss, *Mélanges d'Histoire des Religions* (Paris, 1909), pp. 189 ff.; Ernst Cassirer,
Philosophie der symbolischen Formen, II (1925), ET (New Haven, 1955), pp.
104 ff.; G. van der Leeuw, *Religion in Essence and Manifestation* (London, 1938),
pp. 384 ff.; E. Buess, *Die Geschichte des mythischen Erkennens* (München, 1953),
pp. 143 ff.; C. Tresmontant, *Biblisches Denken und Hellenische Überlieferung*
(Düsseldorf, 1956), pp. 25 ff.; M. Eliade, *The Myth of the Eternal Return*
(ET, New York, 1954); *Patterns in Comparative Religion* (ET, New York,
1958), pp. 388 ff.; G. von Rad, *Theologie des Alten Testaments*, II (München,
1960), pp. 112 ff.

beginning of time. There is no actual distinction in mythical tim
between the past, the present, and the future. Although th
origin of time is projected into the past, to the primeval act c
becoming, this is only a form in which an essentially timeles
reality is clothed. Time is always present and yet to come. I
transcends the modern categories of empirical time. Moreove
mythical time is in no sense an abstraction by which relation
between temporal things are measured in terms of space as, fo
example, 'length of time'. Rather, it is substantialized as a concret
reality which is identical with its content. The character of th
time is measured by the nature of its content. Mythical time i
in no sense homogeneous but, depending upon the quality of
particular time, is designated as holy or profane. It moves in
rhythm of critical periods in which the content of the time waxe
and wanes. The calendar marks these 'times' (*kairoi*) as moment
of primeval power and value. Nevertheless, the oscillation bring
nothing new in essence since the substance remains unchangeable
Its content was determined in the primeval act. In the cultic repe
tition of the myth this act is relived. The power of this event
which fills the content of mythical time, is actualized as the culti
festival becomes the primeval act. The two times sharing the sam
content are therefore identical.

We turn from a general survey of mythical time to a specifi
illustration. It is characteristic of mythical time to conceive o
primeval time as identical with eschatological time (*Urzeit=
Endzeit*). In opposition to modern historical thinking whicl
understands the future as growing out of the past but neve
repeating itself, the myth envisages the future as a return to th
past. There is a complete disregard for chronological time sinc
there is no true beginning or end. 'Jetzt geschieht, was eins
geschah.'[1] Moreover, in the pattern of *Urzeit-Endzeit* nothing
essentially new can ever occur. The decisive act occurs in th
Urzeit as the world's reality is structured. All change is absorbe
into the myth and made part of the timeless past. Apocalypti
Judaism was compelled to speak of a pre-existent temple, a

[1]G. van der Leeuw, 'Urzeit und Endzeit', *Eranos Jahrbuch* (1949), p. 3

Jerusalem (II Bar. 4.2–6) on account of the expectancy of its future return. Finally, this scheme illustrates the mythical understanding of time as moving in a rhythm and being identified with its content. The beginning and end are the times of power *par excellence*. Time is a measure of this content; therefore, the return to the same content indicates also identity of time.

2. *The Biblical Category*

We now intend to examine the Old Testament's understanding of time to see if it shares any features of mythical thinking. Since the entire subject is far too broad for thorough treatment in our study, we will limit our concern to the problem of primeval time as equal to end time.

The probem of *Urzeit-Endzeit* in relation to Old Testament research was originally formulated by Gunkel[1] who followed the pioneer work of Winckler. Research was continued by Gressmann,[2] Dietrich,[3] Schmidt,[4] and many others until the terminology has become common. However, the problem of whether or not the Old Testament shares the mythical pattern of *Urzeit-Endzeit* has had a false element injected into it from the beginning because of an inadequate understanding of the nature of myth. The 'pan-Babylonian' school of Winckler and Jeremias introduced the theory that the essence of the myth was to be found in its cyclic character. Basing their proof chiefly upon Babylonian astrology, they attempted to force this scheme upon myth in general. While we do not doubt that there is in myth a rhythm as we have indicated, it is a later rationalization of this reality, peculiar to certain cultures, which attempted to explain it in terms of a circle. Modern research in mythology has not confirmed the theory that the cycle is central, but that it is only one form which myth takes.[5]

---

[1]H. Gunkel, *Schöpfung und Chaos in Urzeit und Endzeit* (Göttingen, 1895).
[2]H. Gressmann, *Ursprung der israelitisch-jüdischen Eschatologie* (Göttingen, 1905), pp. 160 ff.
[3]E. L. Dietrich, *Schub Schebuth, Die endzeitliche Wiederhestellung bei den Propheten* (BZAW, 40, 1925), pp. 51 ff.
[4]H. Schmidt, *Der Mythus vom wiederkehrenden König im Alten Testament* Berlin, 1925).
[5]Cf. the excellent article of H. Gese, 'Geschichtliches Denken im Alten Orient und im Alten Testament', *ZTK*, 55 (1958), pp. 127 ff.

Because of the introduction of this definition of myth, the problem of whether or not the Old Testament contained the pattern of *Urzeit-Endzeit* was discussed about the issue of whether or not the Old Testament's scheme was 'cyclical' or in some sense 'linear'. Gunkel and Gressmann saw in the Old Testament a sign of cyclical thinking which they labelled mythical. This conclusion was contested by Weiser[1] and Eichrodt[2] who found the cyclic pattern of oriental myth broken by the linear concept of Hebrew eschatology.

It is our opinion that the above controversy has not been correctly formulated, nor have the lines of contention been correctly drawn. In the first place, the definition used of myth is inadequate as we have indicated. Secondly, the concept of 'linear history', so frequently employed as the antithesis of cyclic myth, is not itself a Biblical category, but a rationalization of another sort. The recent scholarship of Robinson,[3] Minear,[4] Marsh, Boman,[6] and Ratschow,[7] continuing the work initiated by Orelli[8] and Pedersen,[9] has been unanimous in stressing that the Hebrew concept of time was primarily interested in the quality of time rather than its temporal succession. The characteristic word for time such as '*ēth* (=LXX *kairos*) and *mô'ēdh* are clearly of this nature. It is the search for the 'right time' which interested the Hebrew (cf. Hag. 1.2; Esther 1.13). The very fact that the Hebrew verbal system indicates qualities of action rather than tenses goes to confirm this analysis. Marsh[10] correctly criticizes Cullmann's

[1] A. Weiser, *Glaube und Geschichte im Alten Testament* (Stuttgart, 1931), pp. 23 ff.

[2] W. Eichrodt, *Theologie des Alten Testaments*, I (5th ed., Göttingen, 1957) pp. 325 f., 336 ff. [ET, Philadelphia and London, 1961, pp. 479f., 494ff.].

[3] H. W. Robinson, *Inspiration and Revelation in the Old Testament* (London 1946), pp. 106 ff.

[4] P. Minear, *Eyes of Faith* (Philadelphia, 1946), pp. 97 ff.

[5] J. Marsh, *The Fulness of Time* (New York–London, 1952), pp. 19 ff.

[6] T. Boman, *Das hebräische Denken im Vergleich mit dem Griechischen* (2nd ed. Göttingen, 1943), pp. 104 ff. [ET, London, 1960, pp. 129 ff.].

[7] C. H. Ratschow, 'Anmerkungen zur theologischen Auffassung des Zeitproblems', *ZTK*, 51 (1954), pp. 360 ff.

[8] C. Orelli, *Die hebräischen Synonyma der Zeit und Ewigkeit* (Leipzig, 1871)

[9] J. Pedersen, *Israel*, I–II (London–Copenhagen, 1926), pp. 486 ff.

[10] Marsh, *op. cit.*, pp. 174 ff.

linear history as a modern abstraction of time expressed in terms of space. The well-known fact that the Hebrew expressed the past in terms of that which was ahead of him (*qdm*), and the future in terms of that which followed (*'ḥr*) illustrates the difference of Hebrew thought from the modern. More recently, however, Eichrodt[1] has criticized the above approach (Marsh, Boman, Ratschow) for failing to do justice to the Biblical understanding of chronological time. He has certainly demonstrated that *chronos* does play a decisive role in Hebrew thinking. The Old Testament registers the passing of successive events in their chronologies and genealogies. Moreover, the eschatological view of a future event toward which all history moves cannot be minimized in importance. Nevertheless, Eichrodt has only succeeded in stressing the role of *chronos* in the Biblical understanding. He has not offered evidence for linear time. It is only in modern categories that the two are identified. To show that the Old Testament prophets looked to the future for the consummation of history is not to disprove the possibility that future and past were identified. The temptation is acute for the *Heilsgeschichte* approach, while contesting the identification of the Biblical view with the mythical, to substitute an identification of the Biblical view with a spiritualized modern theory of history. For these reasons we feel that the question of whether the Old Testament shares the mythical pattern of *Urzeit-Endzeit* (Beginning Time—End Time) must be determined by comparing the Old Testament with the basic categories of mythical time outlined above, rather than by imposing foreign categories of cyclical or linear time.

In our opinion the evidence of an *Urzeit-Endzeit* pattern within Israel is overwhelming.[2] There is to be a returning chaos (Jer. 4.23), a new creation (Isa. 65.17), a new paradise (Amos 9.13 ff.; Isa. 11.6 ff.), and a new covenant of peace between man and beast (Hos. 2.20 (EVV: 2.18); Isa. 11.6 ff.). Moreover, the entire redemptive history of Israel repeats itself in the eschatological age.

---

[1] W. Eichrodt, 'Heilserfahrung und Zeitverständnis im Alten Testament', *TZ*, 12 (1956), pp. 103 ff.
[2] Cf. especially Dietrich, *op. cit.*, pp. 38 ff.

There is to be a redemption again from Egypt and a passing through the sea (Isa. 10.26; Zech. 10.10 f.; Isa. 43.16 f.). The miracles of the wilderness return (Mic. 7.15; Isa. 43.19), a new covenant is established (Jer. 31.31 f.), and a new David will appear who re-establishes his kingdom (Hos. 3.5; Jer. 30.9; Ezek. 34.23). Furthermore, the vocabulary used in these descriptions makes it abundantly clear that the matching of the eschatological events with the past entails far more than a mere device for achieving contrast. The intention is obviously to describe the future as analogical to the past. God will elect Israel 'again' ('*ôdh*, Isa. 14.1; Zech. 1.17). Judah is to be 'rebuilt' (*bānāh*) as it was 'at first' (*bārī'šōnāh*, Jer. 33.7), her 'fortunes returned as once' (*šûbh šĕbhûth*, Amos 9.14 etc.), her children multiplied as in 'the primeval time' (*qedhem*, Jer. 30.20), her cities restored as 'in the days of old' (*kîmê 'ôlām*, Amos 9.11), her sacrifices accepted 'as in ancient years' (*kĕšānîm qadhmoniyyôth*, Mal. 3.4).

In spite of this evidence of the *Urzeit-Endzeit* pattern in the Old Testament, there have been effected some most important alterations in the scheme which must be considered.

i. In the first place, the Old Testament pattern does not conceive of strictly primeval time which returns in end time. We have pointed out that a return of the entire redemptive history of Israel has become the eschatological hope. The primeval acts are considered important only because they form part of Israel's history. This change from the typical mythical pattern signifies a radical alteration on the part of the Old Testament writers regarding their concept of reality. Their witness is that the structure of reality is not determined in a series of primeval acts, but rather a new reality came into being through the redemptive activity of God working in her history. The passing of events marked in chronological time are theologically significant in forming the content of reality. This change in understanding reflects itself in the Hebrew cult. The cult was not a re-enactment of the primeval acts, but an activating of the redemptive acts occurring in chronological time (Deut. 26.5 ff.).

ii. Secondly, the relationship of *Urzeit* to *Endzeit* is not one of imple identity. It cannot be said that, according to the Old Testament, the final act brings nothing essentially new to the primeval act. A study of the concept of 'new' (*ḥdš*) is most revealing in this regard. The root *ḥdš* appears as a common Semitic root with the meaning of 'renew' or 'restore'. The Accadian verb *dēšu* is generally used in regard to restoring ruined temples, cities, or things to a former state.[1] In Ugaritic *ḥdt* appears as a substantive with the characteristic meaning of 'new moon' and also a verb 'to renew the moon'.[2] In Hebrew the verb *ḥdš* has a usage similar to the Accadian, namely to repair an altar (II Chron. 5.8), restore the temple (II Chron. 24.4), renew ruined cities (Isa. 61.4). The face of the ground is renewed (Ps. 104.30), the joy of salvation restored (Ps. 51.12), and the kingdom is renewed (I Sam. 11.14). Lam. 5.21 is specific in expressing the wish for renewal 'as of old'. The usage is especially interesting in Ps. 103.5, 'youth renewed like an eagle', since the reference is very possibly to the fable of the periodic rejuvenation of the eagle. Finally, the usage in Ecclus. 43.8 is reminiscent of the Ugaritic: 'the moon month by month reneweth herself'.

Especially from this latter meaning, the bridge to the substantive *ḥōdheš* (new moon) is easily comprehensible. It is the festival day on which the crescent first reappears, the day of renewal. This latter usage provides the most probable *Sitz-im-Leben* out of which this concept of newness arose. We have here the mythical explanation of the waxing and waning of the moon as a restoring to newness of an original state. The meaning was broadened to apply to other objects, but the sense of restoring to a former condition is basic. In this usage of new, nothing essentially different in quality is implied.

However, in contrast to this usage which lies at the basis of the mythical understanding of time, the Old Testament has another understanding of newness radically different in meaning. It almost seems a conscious attempt at combating the former usage. In the

---

[1] *The Assyrian Dictionary*, vol. 4, ed. A. Leo Oppenheim (Chicago, 1958), p. 30–33.
[2] C. H. Gordon, *Ugaritic Handbook* (Rome, 1947), p. 228, No. 656.

first place this meaning, found chiefly in Deutero-Isaiah, ex
presses a newness appearing in time which differs completely from
any earlier event. Isa. 48.6 speaks of 'new things' (*ḥădhāšôth*)
unknown before, which were 'created now, not long ago'. Isa
42.9 and 43.18 contrast the new thing(s) with former thing
(*rī' šōn*). The former things, in parallel to 'things of old' (43.18 and
in contrast to 'things to come' (41.22), are previous temporal events
The future is to bring new things never before appearing in history
The new is not a mere renewal, but the entrance of the unexpected

In the second place, newness in the Old Testament is expressed
not only in temporal terminology, but also the eschatological hop
of the prophets points to the entrance of a newness differing in
quality from the old. The nature of this quality of newness is mad
clear in Jer. 31.31 ff. The new covenant will not be 'like th
covenant which I made with their fathers'. It is not simply a re
newal of the Sinai covenant as occurred in the yearly festivals
Dietrich's refusal[1] to recognize this element of difference as signi
ficant was obviously dictated by the desire that Israel's pattern cor
respond in all points with the mythical. Jer. 31.32–34 indicate in
what sense the new covenant offers a qualitative difference over th
old. The new covenant, unlike the old which the fathers broke
will be inviolable. God is the author of the old covenant as wel
as the new. There is a continuity in content since from his side th
old covenant remained intact. The newness manifests itself in th
perfect realization of God's original plan. The law had been
accommodated in its form to the sinful condition of the people. I
is at this point that the qualitatively new is accomplished. A
spiritual motivation replaces the external. The sin of the people i
removed and replaced with the right knowledge of God.

A similar example of the qualitatively new is given in Isa
65.17 ff. The new heavens and new earth are contrasted to th
former things (*rī' šōnôth*) which are no longer to be remembered
The world must also be new to harmonize with the new Israel
The description of the new heavens and earth (65.17 ff.) indicate
the author's intention of picturing the entrance of a new realit

[1]Dietrich, *op. cit.*, pp. 41 f.

urpassing the old in every respect. Nevertheless, the new pre-
erves the form of the old. A new Jerusalem is the centre of the
ew world. The original purpose of God with his people is
ccomplished. The removal of sin effects the marvellous extension
f human life. The former curses for disobedience are reversed as
he people live in safety and security in the land. Likewise, a new
eart (Ezek. 18.31), a new song (Isa. 42.10), a new name (Isa.
2.2) are signs of the radically new which has been introduced.

This understanding of newness in the Old Testament has
eriously altered the mythical pattern. Although the *Endzeit* is a
eturn to the *Urzeit*, these two times cannot be simply identified.
according to the Biblical scheme the new can be described as a
eturn and continuance of the old while bringing, at the same
me, a totally different element into being.

iii. Finally, in the Biblical pattern the passing of *chronos* has
ignificance. The mythical pattern of *Urzeit-Endzeit* can ignore
hronological time because the return brings no new content.
dentity of content is also identification of times. But, according
o the Old Testament, the various *kairoi* occur in chronological
me which fills eschatological time with a content unknown to
he primeval time. This is not to be confused with any modern
oncept of time to which a repetition of events is inconceivable.
he two times differing in content are not identical, yet their
ontents are so analogous that they belong together.

In the light of these far-reaching changes in the Biblical use of
he mythical scheme, we should determine whether or not the
cheme *Urzeit-Endzeit* is essentially foreign to the Old Testament's
inking. Is it an inherited framework which the Old Testament
ied to discard? There are two reasons which speak against this
heory. In the first place, there is no sign of internal friction be-
ween the mythical framework and a Biblical content. The pattern
ithin the Old Testament forms a seamless whole with material
hich we know to be indigenous to the Hebrew faith. The friction
xists only with preconceived theories of linear time. Secondly,
e have seen that the Old Testament writers have intentionally
ashioned their material into this pattern. They have altered the

mythical pattern, to be sure, and have shown thereby the freedom
which they felt toward it. The end product bears all the marks of
a freshly created Biblical category, differing from the mythical as
well as the scientific, which we must now attempt to understand

We are now faced with the problem of determining why the
Old Testament used this altered form of the mythical pattern of
Urzeit-Endzeit. Was there a reality which found this form compatible, and then altered it to form a uniquely Biblical category? In
the first place, the return of the eschatological time to the event
of the past indicates that essentially the first and the last form one
event. Although U*rzeit* and *Endzeit* cannot be simply identified
in the myth, they do form a totality. They relate to one another as
the start and end, the beginning and fulfilment of one event. The
pattern indicates that, in the mind of the prophets, these two times
belong to the same *kairos*. They share the same content. The prophetic view of history is undoubtedly teleological, striving toward
the end; nevertheless, the end is conceived of as a return to the
past. In the light of the end time, chronological time is transcended. We do not mean this in the sense of a timeless abstraction,
but according to Hebrew mentality which measures the kind of
time by its content.

Secondly, the altered form of the mythical pattern witnesses to
a reality which appeared first in veiled form, but lastly in its full
intensity. The divine events of redemption in Israel's history were
accommodated in form to the world into which they entered
Although they were signs of a new reality, they partook of the
empirical world, which entailed the possibility of distortion. The
Exodus became the occasion for pride, the Sinai covenant for
legalism, the kingdom for power politics. The prophetic hope of
the new age was pictured in terms of God's former redemptive
acts. However, the last events were now to fulfil the original pur
pose of the first. The return to the past signifies the continuity in
the one will of God; the newness of the end indicates the full
intensity of the light which at first shone only in dim reflection
The new of the *Endzeit* became the criterion for determining what
was qualitatively new at the *Urzeit*.

Thirdly, the category of *Urzeit-Endzeit* strove to express adequately a reality which, although it had already appeared in the past, was still to come in the future. The pattern reflects the tension, especially evident in the prophets, between a present reality and a future hope. Isaiah at his call (Ch. 6) experienced the present kingship of God as the hope for the future. This pattern lays the exegetical basis for sound typological interpretation of the Old Testament. The selfsame divine reality appears past, present and future. The Old Testament deals seriously with these distinctions in chronological time, but the goal of the future as a return to the past demonstrates the oneness of the event in spite of the chronological separation.

In the light of this discussion of the unique function within Israel played by this category, we should finally like to raise the question as to whether or not it can be classified as mythical. Actually, the nomenclature is of secondary importance. We are primarily interested in contrasting the understanding of reality expressed in the mythical and the Hebraic use of this similar pattern.

We have emphasized previously that mythical thinking grew out of a 'two-stage' understanding of the formation of world reality. There was initially a period of non-being. This was superseded by the decisive acts of the primeval age at which time and through which power the world structure was fixed. The purpose of myth was to ensure the continuance of the world's being against all attempts to return to the state of non-being.

The Biblical understanding of reality in contrast to the mythical can be described as 'three-stage'. There was a state of non-being pictured as chaos in the Old Testament. This was overcome by God's gracious acts of creation which brought world reality into being. A third factor was introduced by man's disobedience. A history of sin began which was not a continuation of God's creation put a perversion of reality. The Old Testament recounts the struggle between reality and the perversion of reality. Although the terminology of the 'new' and 'old age' is that of the post-Old Testament writings and of the New Testment, the fundamental distinction is actually present within the Old Testament.

In the obedience of Israel reality takes a shape which transform the old age of perverted reality.

The myth has as its function the maintaining of primeva reality. However, in the Old Testament, that which is classed a mythical has received a new function. It testifies to a new realit which, although present at the primeval time, is eschatological i character. The myth looks to the past, the Old Testament to th future. The reality which the myth wishes to maintain is under stood by the Old Testament as part of the 'old age' and therefor transitory. This difference of attitude toward reality is reflected i the respective cults. The ethnic cult has as its subject the activatin of the primeval acts; the Old Testament cult is a participating i the divine acts of God's redemptive history which is rooted in th past but strives for fulfilment in the future. We conclude tha although the mythical pattern *Urzeit-Endzeit* is shared to a degre by Israel, its function for the Hebrew faith has been entirel altered.

B. THE CONCEPT OF SPACE

1. *An Analysis of Mythical Space*[1]

In contrast to an understanding of the uniformity of space as i Euclidean geometry, mythical space is non-homogeneous i character. While the former conceives of positions within space a determined purely by a neutral relation to each other, mythica space allows a particular content to each position which deter mines what kind of space it is. As with the mythical understand ing of time, space cannot be abstracted from its content. Thi content is afforded to mythical space by the immediate contact o the individual with spatial reality. His sensuous experience fill that particular space with its unique character. By attaching hi experience to certain limited areas, he makes the qualitative distinc tions within space of sacred and profane, each bearing its emo tional character. This scheme is extended beyond the individua experience as cosmic events are also given spatial qualities. Th

[1] The following treatments were the most helpful: Cassirer, *op. cit.*, pp 83 ff.; van der Leeuw, *Religion in Essence*, pp. 393 ff.; Buess, *op. cit.*, pp. 152 ff. M. Eliade, *Patterns in Comparative Religion*, pp. 367 ff.

ole of the myth is central once again in forming this concept of space. The spatial realities, impinging on the sense of man, find the source of their existence in the myth. As an aspect of world reality its origin is projected back to the primeval order. That which is experienced as sacred is a manifestation of the primeval power filling the content of that particular space. Because of the permanence of this sacred content, the cult shares in the primeval power as it enacts its drama in the original space of the primeval act.

Moreover, mythical space is conceived of as a copy of the primeval world structure which shares the same sacred reality. What once came into being is what now exists. The myth relates the decisive act of becoming in terms of personalized divine beings. The structuring of world reality followed the victory of the creator over his evil protagonist. It is characteristic of myth that creation corresponds to the various parts of the body. Sometimes the body is that of the creator's, while at other times that of the defeated enemy. This establishes an ontological correspondence between the world structure and the life of man. The world functions in terms of the human organism. Man's individual life is a microcosm of the universal macrocosm and must be kept in harmony with predetermined reality.

Finally, mythical space conceives of every sign of similarity in the world of reality as an indication of an identity in essence. No matter how separated in space these forms appear the fact that they evidence kinship is cause for their identification. Spaces possessing the same content transcend distance. They are not separate entities, but one reality sharing in primeval power and manifesting the same essence in different forms. In this thinking nothing new can occur or be formed in space which differs essentially from the established structure. Any such change must be denied or absorbed as a primeval act.

2. *The Biblical Category*

Our purpose now is to examine the old Testament traditions concerning Jerusalem and see if there is evidence that a mythical

concept of space is present. It does not take much searching t
discover that Jerusalem possesses a quality which sets it apa
from all other spaces within the world. Zion is a holy place b
cause she belongs to God. There the patriarch, Abraham, had on
prepared to offer Isaac as a sacrifice (II Chron. 3.1; cf. Gen. 22.
14). When the place had been forgotten, the seer Gad, under th
orders of an angel, again pointed out the place to David as ho
(I Chron. 21.18). Here Solomon received a confirmation of fr
at the Temple's dedication (II Chron. 7.1 ff.).

Moreover, Yahweh has chosen Zion to make her his 'restin
place' (*měnûḥāthî*) for ever (Ps. 132.13–14; cf. 125.1; 78.69). F
loves mount Zion (Ps. 78.68) more than the other mountains
Ephraim and there he built his house (87.2). Other mountai
look at Zion in envy since God has singled her out for blessin
(Ps. 68.17). He has made Jerusalem his city and dwells in h
midst (46.6). Therefore is Zion the holy hill (Jer. 31.23), the jc
of the whole earth (Ps. 48.3), the perfection of beauty (Ps. 50.2
Her walls separate the holy space from the common (Ezek. 42.2c
She possesses the cornerstone of the new creation (Isa. 28.16).

Then again, Zion is conceived of as a copy of a heavenly realit
When Yahweh built his sanctuary, he built it like the high heave
(read *kammĕrōnîm* in Ps. 78.69). He established his holy place wi
his hands (Ex. 15.17). Mount Zion he built in the far north (I
48.3), where the 'mount of assembly' was (*bĕhar-mô'ēdh*, Is
14.13). Moreover, he established it 'at the navel of the eart
(Ezek. 38.12; cf. Judg. 9.37). Here we have a clear example
Cassirer's[1] thesis that the world becomes intelligible to th
mythical consciousness by making it analogically 'copied' in terr
of the human body. The credit for having pointed out the sigr
ficance of the term 'navel' belongs primarily to Roscher.[2] Buil
ing on the study of Frazer, he demonstrated convincingly how th
primitive idea of the holiness of the navel assumed cosmologic
significance. Just as the umbilical cord is the source of life for t

[1]Cassirer, *op. cit.*, pp. 90 ff.
[2]W. H. Roscher, *Omphalos* (Leipzig, 1913), pp. 20 ff.; cf. also N.
Omphalosstudien (Leipzig, 1915); *Der Omphalosgedanke bei verschiedenen Völke*
(Leipzig, 1918).

foetus, so the world, conceived of as a flat circular surface, was formed and maintained around the navel.[1]

The work begun by Roscher was continued by Wensinck[2] especially on the basis of Arabic literature. He brought out another motif which occurs in its early form in Isa. 2.2 ff. and played such an important role in the later prophetic and apocalyptic literature. The sanctuary as the navel of the world, resting on the top of the mountains, becomes the place of communication with both the heavenly and nether worlds.[3] Klameth[4] and Jeremias[5] have pursued the development of the idea of the navel in Jewish and Christian thought.

Jerusalem as the navel of the earth is also the heavenly city[6] come to earth. Her walls and gates are built of precious stones (Isa. 54.11 ff.). The introduction in Ezek. 40.1–4 removes all doubt that Jerusalem is envisioned as a copy of the heavenly city. This theme received its widest elaboration in the Apocrypha. In Tobit 13.16–17 the city is described as having gates of sapphire and walls of pure gold. Following the destruction of Jerusalem the frequency of this motif was increased (II (4) Esd. 7.26; 10:54–59; 13.36; II Bar. 4.2–6).

Finally, there is evidence of the mythical understanding of space in the identification of Zion with Eden. When two spaces possess the same content, then distance is transcended. These are not two different spaces, but one. Isaiah pictures the primeval harmony of Eden as part of future Zion (11.6 ff.). Deutero-Isaiah sees the wilderness of Zion turned into a garden like Eden (51.3).

---

[1]Cf. the most recent discussion and bibliography of G. Lanczkowski, 'Nabel', *RGG³*, vol. IV, *loc. cit.*

[2]A. J. Wensinck, *The Ideas of the Western Semites concerning the Navel of the Earth* (1916), pp. 11 f.

[3]*Ibid.*, p. 30.

[4]G. Klameth, *Die Neutestamentlichen Lokaltraditionen Palästinas*, I (München, 1914), pp. 88 ff.

[5]J. Jeremias, *Golgotha* (Leipzig, 1926), pp. 40 ff.

[6]Cf. H. Gressmann, *The Tower of Babel* (New York, 1928), pp. 56 ff.; A. Causse, 'Le Mythe de la nouvelle Jérusalem du Deutéro-Esaie à la IIIe Sibylle', *RHPR*, 18 (1938), pp, 377 ff.; G. von Rad, *EvTh*, 8 (1948–9), pp. 439 ff.; K. L. Schmidt, 'Jerusalem als Urbild und Abbild', *Eranos Jahrbuch*, 18 (1950), pp. 207 ff.

The long life of the *Urzeit* returns to Jerusalem with the fruitfulness of the restored land (Isa. 32.15 ff.; 65.17 ff.). Ezek. 47.1 ff.
describes a stream which issues forth from below the threshold of
the Temple and rapidly increases until it becomes a mighty river,
flowing down to the Dead Sea. This is no ordinary water; rather,
from its effects we see that it is the life-giving water of the garden
of Paradise. Instead of the 'Dead Sea', there is now a lake teeming
with fish. On the banks spring up the trees of paradise, magical
trees which bear fresh fruit every month (47.12). In their leaves
there is healing for the sick. Joel's description (4.18 ff.—EVV:
3.18 ff.) of the restored fruitfulness is reminiscent of Amos 9.11 ff.

Moreover, both Zion and Eden are pictured as the world-
mountain at the centre of the earth. Already in Gen. 2.10–14 there
was a tradition which conceived of Eden as the source of the four
world rivers encircling the earth. Ezekiel draws from a similar
tradition when he describes Eden as a 'holy mountain of God'
(28.13 f.). In the light of these passages the prophetic description
of Zion as a world-mountain receives its full significance. Zion
has become Eden. Instead of being only some 2,500 feet high, it
has become the highest of the mountains, reaching up into the
heavens, towering over all the creation around it. Zechariah has a
similar picture of the future Jerusalem elevated over all the land
(14.10). Many of the other paradise motifs return in this passage.
The radical transformation of the new age abolishes the seasons
and the change of day. Whereas Ezekiel 47 has the water flowing
only to the east, we have mention in Zech. 14.8 of living water
which waters the land both east and west.

In Ps. 48.3 there appears the same picture of Zion being elevated above the rest of the world, but in this passage another
motif is mentioned which is only implicit in Isaiah 2, namely,
'Mount Zion, in the extreme north'. In the Old Testament this
term has an ambivalent meaning.[1] The north can be the direction
out of which the demonic enemy descends (Jer. 4.6, etc.),[2] or it can

[1]Cf. especially A. Lauha, *Zaphon, Der Norden und die Nordvölker im Alten
Testament* (Helsinki, 1943).
[2]B. S. Childs, 'The Enemy from the North and the Chaos Tradition', *JBL*,
78 (1959), pp. 187 ff.

e the source of blessing, the seat of the deity. The phrase appears
ith this latter connotation in Isa. 14.13 where we hear of the
mount of assembly in the far north'. Gressmann[1] had suggested
he Canaanite background of this idea even before the discovery
f the Ras Shamra texts. Since their discovery there can be little
oubt that the idea of the world-mountain in the north stems
ltimately from Canaanite mythology. The term 'north' in its
rimary sense is to be understood locally as referring to the
ountain Zaphon,[2] seat of the chief Canaanite god, Baal Zaphon.
Moreover, it is easy to see how the idea of a world-mountain arose
n the light of Eissfeldt's location of the mountain. Mons Casius,
he present *jebel 'el-'akra'*, is 1770 metres high and dominates
orthern Syria. In this passage the future Zion is painted
ith mythological pictures stemming from old Canaanite
radition.

Our investigation has shown that concepts such as 'world-
mountain', 'mountain in the north', 'navel of the earth', have been
orrowed by the Hebrews chiefly from Canaanite mythology.
However, the significant thing for our study is that the identical
ictures have been used to describe both Eden and Zion. It seems,
herefore, evident that in the mind of the Biblical writers, Eden
nd Zion were not clearly distinguished. Rather, a mythical con-
ept of space appears in this identification. Since their quality of
pace was the same, the two could be identified.

We should like to summarize briefly the evidence we have just
resented that Zion is conceived of in the Old Testament in terms
f mythical space. The main characteristics in mythical thinking
bout space are clearly present. Zion has a quality of holiness
hich sets it apart from all other 'common' space. Moreover,
ion as a copy of the heavenly reality is pictured in terms of the
uman body. The world functions as an organism with Zion as its
avel. Finally, there is an identification of Zion, with Eden. Be-
ause both share the same quality of sacred space, distance is

---

[1]Gressmann. *Der Messias,* p. 169.
[2]Eissfeldt, *Baal Zaphon, Zeus Kaison, und der Durchzug der Israeliten durchs
eer* (Halle, 1932), pp. 5 ff.

transcended. Since God first created Eden as his sacred place, an
other space partaking of this holiness must be Eden.

While we have pointed out the signs of a mythical understanding
of space regarding Zion, there is also evidence to show that in
important places within the Old Testament the mythical pattern
has been altered. In the first place, Zion is not a holy place estab
lished in the *Urzeit* as part of God's initial creation. Rather, it only
became a holy place in the course of Israel's history. It belongs to
part of the history of David's rise to the throne that he chose
Jerusalem as the site for his capital (II Sam. 6). The institution of
the Temple came into being as part of the historical development
of Israel.[1] The attempts to disregard the historical nature of Zion
and force the institution into a mythical framework can only be
done by disregarding the evidence. For example, Gressmann sug
gests that perhaps there was a tradition in Israel of Yahweh estab
lishing as his first act of creation his holy mountain.[2] This sug
gestion follows logically from the mythical concept of space. If a
place were holy, then it must derive its content from a primeval act
However, Gressmann's suggestion cannot be substantiated in
Israel. It is exactly at this point that Israel broke the mythical frame
work. The establishing of Zion is an historical, not a mythical event

It is of interest to note that in later Judaism there is a definite
development toward the mythologizing of Zion at the expense of
the historical. II Baruch 4.2–4 speaks of a pre-existent Jerusalem
formed before the creation of Paradise which God showed to
Adam before he sinned. From the primeval Rock the world was
created.[3] Adam, Cain and Abel, and Noah all offered sacrifice
at the sanctuary.[4] Adam was buried on the holy mountain.

[1]H.-J. Kraus, *Die Königsherrschaft Gottes im Alten Testament* (Tübingen
1951), pp. 34 ff.; *Gottesdienst in Israel* (München, 1954), p. 73; Martin Noth
'Jerusalem und die israelitische Tradition,' *Oudtestamentische Studiën,* VII
(1950), pp. 28 ff.

[2]Gressmann, *Der Messias,* p. 171.

[3]Yoma 54b (Bar.), cited by Jeremias, *op. cit.,* p. 54.

[4]Adam: Palestinian Targum on Gen. 8.20; Cain and Abel: Pirqe Rabb
Eliezer 23 (in G. Friedlander's translation, London, 1916, 171); Noah: Pirq
Rabbi Eliezer 31 (Friedlander, 227);—cited from Jeremias, *ibid.,* p. 24.

[5]Jeremias, *ibid.,* p. 39.

It was at this holy place that Jacob saw the ladder reaching up into the heavens.[1] Moreover, the significant thing for our present study is the fact that this process of mythologizing of Israel's history had already begun in the book of Chronicles. The effort is made to relate Israel's entire *Heilsgeschichte* to the one holy place. I Chron. 22.1 identifies the threshing floor of Ornan the Jebusite with the holy place on which the Temple was to be erected, thus linking David more closely than ever with Zion. The emphasis has shifted from that of II Sam. 6 since David, according to the Chronicler, no longer chooses Zion to make it a holy place. It has always had that character. The angel with the stretched sword confirms its holiness which has merely been rediscovered by David. Then again, II Chron. 3.1 identifies Jerusalem with Mount Moriah, linking the patriarchs Abraham and Isaac with Zion. This mythical tendency within later Judaism to project Zion back into the *Urzeit* and reinterpret history to reflect its central role only goes to emphasize the non-mythological character of the original Zion tradition.

There is a second change in contrast to the purely mythical concept of space which is closely allied to the Hebrew understanding of history. While Zion is pictured as a manifestation of Eden, there is never a simple identification between the two as in the myth. At times the prophets relate Zion to Eden analogically: 'The Lord . . . will make her (Zion's) wilderness *like* Eden, her deserts like the garden of Yahweh' (Isa. 51.3). Moreover, even in the many instances previously mentioned in which Zion assumed directly all the characteristics of Eden, there is not the simple identification basic to the myth. Instead, the content of Zion has been filled with new elements not present in the *Urzeit*. Zion is the site of the Temple, the sanctuary of God's chosen people, the holy city of King David. It is central to the Hebrew concept of God's revelation in history that these historically conditioned institutions are not assimilated by projecting them back into the beginning. The processes of history are viewed as producing something new over and above the sacred space of the primeval age.

[1]Genesis Rabba 77, in Jeremias, *ibid.*, p. 24.

Finally, the mythical understanding of sacred space as possess
ing an unchangeable quality of holiness was emphatically rejected
by the Hebrew prophets. According to myth, a space is holy when
it possessed the primeval power of the *Urzeit* released at creation.
Myth does allow a rhythmic fluctuation in the intensity with which
a sacred place participates in the primeval power, and therefore it
is the function of the cult to reactivate this latent power. The
prophets, however, rejected this mythical understanding of sacred
space. Holiness is not an impersonal force stemming from a primeval act, but that which belongs to the covenant God and shares his
being. A place is never holy apart from its relation to Yahweh. It
can possess no permanent quality of holiness. The content of space
is determined by its relationship to Yahweh rather than an inherent quality of the sacred. Isaiah contrasts the true holiness of
Zion as acknowledged in faith with the false confidence in empirical Jerusalem which will be swept away (Isa. 28.14 ff.). Because
Zion has been 'built with blood and Jerusalem with wrong' the
prophet Micah announces its total destruction (3.10 ff.). Likewise
Jeremiah attacks the current opinion of the inviolability of sacred
Jerusalem. The Temple has become a 'den of robbers' and will be
devastated as completely as Shiloh (7.1 ff.). According to Ezekiel
Jerusalem is only the holy city when the glory of Yahweh is
present (Chs. 9-11; 43-44). The prophets, therefore, by reinter-
preting sacred space theologically with definite ethical implications
effected a radical departure from the mythical concept of space.

We have attempted to demonstrate up to this point that the
Old Testament makes use of a mythical concept of space—but in
a form which has been altered at decisive points. Now we should
ask ourselves what purpose was behind the selection of this
particular category. Did the Biblical writers find in the altered
mythical pattern a compatible vehicle by which to bear witness to
a new reality? We should like to suggest, in the first place, that
the mythical concept of space was useful to the Biblical writers in
emphasizing the *quality* of space rather than the location. It is the
kind of space which is of primary interest to the Old Testament
prophets. Both Eden and Zion share the same quality of space

Both Eden and Zion are described as places where a complete harmony exists between God and his creation. Here is a space which belongs to God and reflects his rule. In contrast to the fallen world, a new creation has appeared and entered into space. Zion can be pictured in terms of Eden because they both are special manifestations of one reality, the new creation.

Secondly, the mythical concept of space in its Biblical form offers testimony to a spatial reality which appeared at the beginning of history and which continued to manifest itself throughout Israel's history. The myth indicates that that which appeared in Zion is not new, but already manifest in Eden. Moreover, the future Zion is described in terms of the garden of Eden to testify that even that which the latter days bring is part of the new creation already known. The continuity of God's redemptive acts as participating in the spatial reality of the same new creation is given clear expression in the broken myth. However, the mythical form was altered in the Old Testament, since it did not do justice in its unbroken state to the acts of God in history as the revelation of his new creation. The new elements found in the description of Zion but not present in Eden indicate the further historical manifestation of God's new creation in space. The future Zion is not a simple return to Eden. The history of Israel is the account of God's redemptive acts occurring in space. Because of man's sin this reality was veiled. Zion, which was to be the spatial sign of God's rule over his redeemed people, soon became the means through which sinful Israel sought security. The new Jerusalem, pictured in terms of Eden, is the prophetic assurance that the future will fulfil that which was begun in the past.

Finally, we would like to conclude this discussion by comparing the role which the category of mythical space plays in the unbroken myth with its purpose in the Old Testament. It is our contention that, in spite of the great similarity in the structure of the spatial category, their respective roles are essentially different in purpose. The myth attempts to understand spatial reality in terms of the present world order which is conceived of as occurring in a primeval act, overcoming the world of non-being. The kind of space which came into being received its content at thi time. The essence of sacred space cannot be altered, but is main tained and reactivated by the cult which relives the act of creation This mythical category of space reflects a world view which con ceives of reality as a static unchangeable substance, indee fluctuating in a rhythmic pattern, but always having for its goal return to the past.

In contrast, the Old Testament category of space, while adopt ing a quasi-mythical form, was used basically to express a differen concept of reality. The Old Testament understood spatial realit in terms of a new creation which was not to be identified with either the present world order or the world of non-being. God in history was bringing into existence a new spatial reality analogous to the new temporal reality. It was not divorced from the present world of space but differed in the quality of its space The history of Israel is the history of God's new space entering into the world of the 'old space', and its being rejected and mis understood. The prophetic hope looked to the future when th reality of the new creation already experienced would come in it fullness. Isaiah heard the liturgy of the seraphim announcing 'the whole earth is full of his glory'. His message became proclamation of judgment on man's unholy creation and of re demptive hope for the consummation of a reality already diml perceived.

The Old Testament's understanding of space was eschato logical, not mythical. It looked to the future, not to the pas However, it chose a mythical category to express the tension within this new spatial reality. The new space had as its conter God's holiness, but it was formed in the midst of a profane an fallen space. This space had already appeared, but was yet to com in its fullness.

V

THE THEOLOGICAL PROBLEM OF MYTH

A. SUMMARY OF THE RESULTS OF OUR EXEGESIS

We should like to summarize briefly the results of our study before attempting to draw theological implications. The problem of the myth within the Old Testament was clearly formulated for the first time by H. Gunkel. In contrast to the drawing of arbitrary parallels of the ancient oriental myths with Biblical passages, as was practised in his day, Gunkel developed a sound and scientific approach to the study of myth within the Old Testament. He perfected the method of tracing with a high degree of objectivity the process by which mythical material entered Israel's tradition and was gradually assimilated. As early as 1895 in his epoch-making book, *Schöpfung und Chaos,* Gunkel demonstrated on the basis of the creation myth the process by which Israel demythologized myth.

However, in spite of the unparalleled clarity with which he described the various stages through which the process of demythologizing passed, there were two problems which, in our opinion, were not satisfactorily solved by him or his successors. It has been the purpose of this study to shed light on these two questions.

1. In the first place, Gunkel never penetrated beyond the formal side in understanding *how* the process of demythologizing took place in Israel. Although he traced with accuracy the change which the mythical material underwent, his chief interest lay in reconstructing the earliest stage of myth. This tendency becomes especially evident in his commentary on Genesis. The actual process by which Israel struggled to overcome myth never received his full attention. Rather, he characterized Israel's effort to

95

assimilate as stemming merely from a monotheistic aversion to myth.[1] Thus whenever mythical fragments retained themselves in the Hebrew tradition, Gunkel concluded that it was a sign of an undigested particle resisting the forward development of monotheism.

Our approach to this problem has not been to postulate a goal of monotheism, but rather to start with Israel's basic understanding of reality. Using this as our key we have tried to show the exact nature of Israel's struggle. A criterion has been developed for measuring the different degrees of control with which Israel assimilated the mythical material. This we did in terms of the friction produced between the Biblical understanding of reality and the mythical. Passages such as Gen. 1.2 and Gen. 3.1–5, which Gunkel described as a 'treasury of mythical vestiges', under close scrutiny revealed a high degree of theological understanding in skilled assimilation. In other passages where far less control was evidenced, we pointed out the decisive points at which the demythologizing process had set in. Moreover, our study indicated elements within the mythical material which proved to be compatible vehicles for re-use by the Biblical writers. The broken myth within Israel's tradition cannot be judged merely negatively as part of a primitive stage in development, but it served a unique purpose in communicating the Biblical understanding of reality.

2. In the second place, Gunkel did not deal adequately with the theological problem of *why* myth was demythologized in Israel. This failure stemmed ultimately from his basic theological presuppositions. Standing in the romantic tradition of Herder, he conceived it as his task merely to reproduce in unbroken form Israel's archaic and primitive traditions. He understood Israel's history as a 'history of piety' (*Frömmigkeitsgeschichte*) to which the modern reader had access only through an aesthetic participation.[2] We believe that these categories prevented him from raising the

[1] Gunkel, *Genesis* (4th ed.), pp. xiv f.
[2] Cf. the excellent analysis of H.-J. Kraus, *Geschichte der historisch-kritischen Erforschung des Alten Testaments von der Reformation bis zur Gegenwart* (Neukirchen, 1956), pp. 300 ff.

central theological problems of the myth. Our purpose has been to demonstrate that Israel succeeded in overcoming the myth because of an understanding of reality which opposed the mythical. Our exegesis has sought to point out the highly theological nature of the struggle evidenced in such passages as Gen. 3.1–5 and 6.1–4. Moreover, our study has attempted to throw light on the role of the myth in forming theological categories to express the uniquely Biblical concepts of time and space by which Israel gave articulation to her understanding of the new reality.

B. THE THEOLOGICAL PROBLEM

Finally, it is time to draw from this study some theological conclusions, which we hope will contribute to the contemporary discussion regarding the problem of reality in the Bible. The central question can be formulated as follows: 'What is the nature of the reality of which the Bible is a witness?' We shall approach the problem from the standpoint of Biblical theology. We are well aware of the broader problem of systematic theology as presented, for example, in P. Tillich's *Biblical Religion and the Search for Ultimate Reality* (1955) in which he attempts to relate the Biblical understanding of reality to an ontological analysis of the structure of being. This problem of systematic theology lies beyond the scope of this discussion. We are restricting ourselves to the problem of reality within the Bible, although we feel that the Biblical material which we present can, in turn, be used by the systematic theologian in seeking an answer to his broader problem.

1. *The New Reality in the Old Testament is 'New Israel'*

The new reality of which the Bible speaks has taken shape within historical Israel. The Old Testament recounts the story of the people of Israel. It saw in her concrete historical situations which were fixed in particular times, restricted to limited geographical areas, and focussed on a special people, God's bringing into being a new kind of existence. In the historical development of the Hebrew people, the Old Testament conceived of the entrance into the world of a new factor. It explained this people's total

existence in terms of an encounter with the covenant God of
Israel, who in the Exodus had created them into a people, who in
the conquest of Palestine had provided them with a home, and
who through the covenant had given them their institutions. Israel
knew God only in the forms in which they had experienced him.

We are emphazising that the reality of which the Bible speaks
took form within the life of historical Israel, but what is the
reality? In our opinion, the message of the Old Testament is that
the reality is the 'New Israel'. Obedient and faithful Israel is the
new existence. The Old Testament consistently placed the initia-
tive for redemptive action on the side of God; however, it stressed
that only as there was an obedient response was there a new
reality. There was no abstract knowledge of this reality, but in the
concrete acts of justice and mercy to one's fellows one partici-
pated in it. When the prophets attempted to describe the nature of
the life pleasing to God, it was always in terms of covenantal
obedience. God's redemptive purpose in the world was seen only
in the tangible shape of the Israel who did justice, loved kindness,
and walked humbly with her God.

The Old Testament conceived of the experiences of Israel as the
process by which God brought into being a new form of existence.
Our study of the myth attempted to demonstrate the manner in
which these people who had experienced the new reality expressed
themselves in destroying foreign mythology. They could not
tolerate the concept of reality found in the myth since it opposed
that new reality of which they were a part. In a similar way, Israel
expressed her new life by transforming all her institutions as well
as her traditions in such a way as to bring them into conformity
with her concept of reality. However, the Old Testament is also
a history of Israel's rejection of the new way of life. It is a story of
the manner in which the old forms of existence fought to ex-
tinguish the new. There is no 'upward sloping line' of gradual
perfection, but the Old Testament ends in dissidence. Because of
the inability of the new existence to maintain itself within Israel,
the Old Testament is theologically meaningless apart from the
New Testament.

When we link the reality of which the Old Testament speaks with the total experience of Israel, we are thereby making some important claims regarding the nature of this reality. We are affirming that that which is ultimate in the Old Testament has been inextricably tied to the forms of Israel's daily life, including her history, tradition, institutions, thought-patterns, and language. Biblical reality is not found in some external divine action. There are no 'objective events' which can be divorced from the particular colouring of Israel. We cannot penetrate 'behind' Israel to find reality. Only as it is reflected in the experience of this people do we have access to it. Only through a study of the particulars of Hebrew civilization can the reality about which the Old Testament is concerned be understood. Even beyond this, the claim of reality appearing in Israel carries with it the important implication that it cannot be separated from its particular historical manifestation. In spite of the limitation and ambiguity of every historically conditioned entity, the new form of existence has taken shape in such concrete form that any attempt to abstract the eternal from the temporal or to distinguish between the form and the content destroys the reality.

2. *Our Position Contrasted with Other Approaches*

The position which we have been developing regarding the Biblical understanding of reality can be further clarified by briefly contrasting it with the approach of several contemporary theologians. We have suggested that Biblical reality be understood as the 'New Israel' which took concrete form within historical Israel. We have set the new reality within the context of Israel's total experience. We feel that it is highly significant to link reality with this *total expression* of historical Israel rather than to connect reality with any one aspect of Israel's life whether it be with ideas or with historical elements within her tradition. Reality is to be found in Israel and not in an abstraction or restriction of this concrete manifestation. We encounter it only in the whole articulation which Israel gave of herself. The 'offence' of Israel cannot be avoided by going behind her experience or spiritualizing it. In

99

our opinion, the failure of modern Biblical theology to reach a successful solution to this problem stems from the attempt to relate reality to something other than the concrete experience of Israel. Usually this has taken the form of finding reality in the *ideas* of Israel or in some *concept* of history into which certain aspects of Israel's life can be fitted. We will try to illustrate this by reference to several important attempts at a solution to this same problem.

a. Classical Liberalism arose following the impact of historical criticism on the Bible. It was generally accepted that the orthodox position of claiming absolute historicity for every event recorded in the Bible had become untenable. Liberalism attempted by means of an idealistic philosophy to retain the ultimate value of the Bible. It distinguished between 'abiding truths' and 'temporal trappings'. These truths in terms of ideas could then be abstracted from the limitations of their Biblical settings. Certainly the Liberal approach made a genuine contribution in trying to take seriously the 'subjective' side of Israel's experience as a medium of reality. However, the weakness of defining reality in terms of mere ideas divorced from the historical Israel who formulated them has been repeatedly emphasized in our day.

b. More recently the problem of understanding Biblical reality has taken the form of trying to relate Biblical reality to varying concepts of history.[1] This has usually necessitated a redefining of

[1] The recent literature on the problem of history is vast. The following works have proved helpful to the author: A. Weiser, *Glaube und Geschichte im Alten Testament* (Stuttgart, 1931); C. H. Dodd, *History and the Gospel* (London 1938), pp. 11–38; O. Piper, *God in History* (New York, 1939); W. F. Albright *From the Stone Age to Christianity* (2nd ed. Baltimore, 1946), pp. 48–87 P. S. Minear, *Eyes of Faith* (Philadelphia, 1946); M. Buber, *Moses* (ET London, 1946), pp. 13–19; Amos Wilder, 'Heilsgeschichte and the Bible' *Christendom*, XIII (1948), pp. 10 ff.; G. von Rad, 'Theologische Geschichts-schreibung im Alten Testament', *TZ*, 4 (Basel, 1948), pp. 161 ff.; W. Eich-rodt, 'Offenbarung und Geschichte im Alten Testament', *TZ*, 4 (1948) pp. 321 ff.; O. Cullmann, *Christ and Time* (ET; London, 1951); P. S. Minear 'Between Two Worlds', *Interpretation*, V (1951), pp. 27 ff.; Robert Pfeiffer 'Facts and Faith in Biblical History', *JBL*, 70 (1951), pp. 1 ff.; G. Ernest Wright, *God Who Acts* (London, 1952); B. Davie Napier, *From Faith to Faith* (New York, 1955); M. Burrows, 'Ancient Israel', *The Idea of History in the Ancient Near East*, ed. R. Dentan (New Haven, 1955), pp. 101 ff.; H.-J Kraus, 'Das Problem der Heilsgeschichte in der "Kirchlichen Dogmatik" ' *Antwort* (Zollikon, 1956), pp. 69 ff.; F. Hesse, 'Die Erforschung der Geschicht

the common meaning of history in an effort to break the impasse reached by the orthodox and Liberal attempts. Rudolf Bultmann, for example, redefines history in terms of '*Geschichte*' and '*Historie*'. *Geschichte* is the event in which man is involved existentially, while *Historie* is history joined in an immanental cause and effect relationship and subject to historical criticism.[1] Bultmann attempts to relate Biblical reality to existential history, thus removing reality from the sphere of historical criticism, while at the same time seeking to retain the event character of Biblical reality. Modern theology is much indebted to his insights in attempting to free reality from the restrictions of historicism and yet preserve the event character of man's encounter with reality. However, Bultmann's existential history has become a very pale and emaciated kind of history devoid of genuine historical earthiness. Ott characterizes it as having lost the genuine 'corporeality' of history (*Unleiblichkeit*).[2] We wonder also in Bultmann's existential history what the role is of the community in relation to reality.

O. Cullmann's book, *Christ and Time* (ET 1951), severely criticizes Bultmann's concept of history as having lost the characteristics of truly Biblical history which he feels is linear time. In his careful study Cullmann also accepts a distinction between *Geschichte* and *Historie*. The former term he reinterprets in terms of God's redemptive history which moves in linear time toward its eschatological consummation. We feel that Cullmann has rendered a valuable service in pointing out the theological significance of chronological time, without which there can be no real history. Nevertheless, as we have pointed out previously in this study, it is extremely doubtful whether the concept of time in the

---

als theologische Aufgabe', *KeDo*, 4(1958), pp. 1 ff.; J. Coert Rylaarsdam, 'The Problem of Faith and History in Biblical Interpretation', *JBL*, 77 (1958), pp. 26 ff.; J. Hempel, 'Die Faktizität der Geschichte im Biblischen Denken', *Biblical Studies in Memory of H. C. Alleman* (Locust Valley, N.Y., 1960), pp. 67 ff.; *Offenbarung als Geschichte*, ed. W. Pannenberg (Göttingen, 1961).

[1] For a comprehensive analysis of Bultmann's concept of history, cf. H. Ott, *Geschichte und Heilsgeschichte in der Theologie Rudolf Bultmanns* (Tübingen, 1955).
[2] *Ibid.*, p. 176.

Bible is actually linear. We would also wonder whether Cullmann's *Geschichte* has not become a type of abstraction devoid of
the true characteristics of history. Is it not to deal with history
symbolically when one talks of *Geschichte* 'occurring', but not
entering into the area of historical measurability?

Karl Barth objects to the above attempts to develop a theory
of history first and then to apply it to the Biblical revelation.
He is also critical of defining history in terms of *Geschichte*
and *Historie* lest the Biblical reality be consigned merely to a
history of religion. Barth defines history in terms of God's execu-
tion of his purpose through his Word (which is Jesus Christ) in
bringing to completion his covenant of grace.[1] Barth avoids the
dangers of a dualistic concept of history by remaining strictly
within the Biblical categories. Although he attempts to do justice
theologically to history, in practice his history also tends to lose
its earth-bound qualities. Barth certainly acknowledges historical
criticism, but its findings are consigned merely to formal matters
without adding any tangible content to his history. One can
seriously question whether Barth has solved the problem of
history or merely avoided it.

In our opinion, these three attempts to understand the reality
of which the Bible witnesses by means of redefining history
although differing greatly from one another, all share a certain
abstraction which has sacrificed the concrete nature of the Biblical
reality.

c. To avoid this abstraction of history G. Ernest Wright
suggests grounding an Old Testament *Heilsgeschichte* upon 'out-
ward, objective happenings of history'.[2] He links the Biblical
reality to Israel's concrete history which has been empirically
validated. From these events 'inferences' of faith are drawn. This
method has certainly avoided the pitfalls of abstraction. A genuine
history of Israel appears with its rich diversity. However, we would
raise the question as to whether there is another danger inherent
in this approach. Can the reality of which the Old Testament

[1] Karl Barth, *Die Kirchliche Dogmatik,* III-1, pp. 63 ff. [ET. pp. 59 ff.].
[2] G. Ernest Wright, *op. cit.,* p. 55.

speaks be restricted to 'objective history'? Is this an attempt to penetrate behind Israel's formulation of her experience to the 'real events'? Does not this approach allow historical criticism to restrict the realm into which reality can appear? Then again, can the witness of the Bible to reality be divided into subjective and objective portions on the basis of criticism? We feel that the theological objections to the 'search for the historical Jesus' can also be applied to this search for the 'historical Israel'.

3. *The Theological Implications of Our Approach to Reality*

We suggest that these various pitfalls which have hindered an understanding of Biblical reality can be avoided by turning from abstraction, whether philosophical or historical, to the concrete expressions of Israel's life. By rejecting modern categories in a search to find reality, we are made receptive to Israel's own categories by which she expressed her existence. In saga, in legend, the broken myth, through these unhistorical vehicles as well as through the historical, Israel articulated her understanding of her existence. Since the new reality has taken concrete form in the life of Israel, reality is tied to every part of her total life, not just to the events possessing confirmed historicity. The Old Testament's 'history of redemption' (*Heilsgeschichte*) is the life of Israel. The demythologizing of mythological traditions which we have traced is also a definite part of this history. Naturally, it is our decision of faith whether or not we want to take our standpoint with Israel and see her experience as a genuine encounter *with God* rather than just an encounter with herself.

The approach we are suggesting, furthermore, destroys the false antithesis which has been set up frequently between the subjective and the objective portions of the Biblical witness. The reality with which the Old Testament is concerned is anchored to the totality of Israel. Reality is not found in historical happenings which impinge from above upon Israel and to which she subsequently adds subjective reflection. All such distinctions do not take seriously the fact that God has made himself known in the total experience of Israel. In the memory, consciousness, and reflections of Israel, Old Testament *Heilsgeschichte* has taken place. The Old Testament contains a history only because Israel gave her experiences a coherent formulation. In our opinion, this is the only theologically responsible way to deal with the Biblical tradition. The development in the creation account as recorded in the Priestly tradition in contrast to the earlier expression of the Yahwist cannot be dismissed as 'subjective accretion', but must be evaluated as an expression of Israel's new life.

This leads to the problem of historical criticism and its relation to the reality of the Bible. We feel that by linking the new reality to the total life of historical Israel, historical criticism can be employed with full seriousness. Through historical research we have been given a means to reconstruct the life of this ancient people. By disavowing the use of any dualistic concept of history, we have recovered the unity of history with its tangible, earthbound qualities. The more comprehensive the picture of historical Israel becomes, the more complete will be our understanding of the reality for which the Old Testament is concerned. We have made room for genuine historical research as the indispensable tool of theology.

However, historical criticism can by no means restrict the Biblical reality. It cannot limit this reality to any particular historical form. The new reality is not tied to the historicity of Biblical events. Historical criticism has as its purpose the reconstructing of a comprehensive picture of the past with the highest degree of accuracy possible. It determines the historicity of events recorded, and classifies the material into its various literary forms of historical biography, myth, saga, etc. It discovers those events which have a solid historical foundation as well as those which stem chiefly from the inner life of the community of Israel. It traces the historical processes by which Israel grew, developed, and declined. In other words, historical criticism is a descriptive science. With its tools it cannot pass a value judgment on the reality to which the Bible addresses itself. The new reality of the Old Testament, which is obedient and faithful Israel, obviously cannot be measured in terms of historicity.

What then is the criterion for determining the new reality within the Old Testament since historical criticism is incapable of passing this judgment? We have described the reality with which the Old Testament is concerned as the 'New Israel', formed within the concrete historical life of the Hebrew people. How can the 'New Israel' be distinguished from the 'Old Israel'? According to the entire Old Testament witness there are no general ethical principles or 'right doctrines' by which the new existence can be measured. Such foreign categories do only injustice to the Old Testament. We are forced to discover inner Biblical categories. Within the Old Testament one can see growth and change, both regarding Israel's understanding of God and of herself. It is an important task of the exegete on the basis of the whole Old Testament canon to see wherein the chief emphases of the Old Testament faith lie. However, the criterion for reality cannot be in terms of importance in Israel's faith. At this juncture the Christian makes his confession of faith. The ultimate criterion for determining the new reality does not lie within the Old Testament. In Jesus Christ *the* new reality has appeared as the self-authenticating 'New Israel'. As the truly obedient man Jesus is the new existence in its fullest and most concrete form. 'Indeed, an Israelite in whom there is no guile.' Not just in his teachings or in particular actions, but in the total existence of the Jew, Jesus Christ, the entire Old Testament receives its proper perspective. It is fulfilled in its obedience, but judged in its disobedience.

Finally, we feel that our understanding of reality in terms of the 'New Israel' clarifies many of the problems regarding the relation of the two Testaments. The Christian Church retained the Old Testament not for antiquarian reasons, but because it spoke of Jesus Christ. The Old Testament is not just an historical preparation for his coming, but it is a manifestation of him. Yet every time the attempt has been made to determine more precisely the presence of Jesus Christ within the Old Testament, Jesus emerges as a very shadowy figure and the Old Testament loses its real content. This uncertainty appears not only in the Biblical theologies, but reflects itself even more acutely in the pulpits of the

Christian Church. In our opinion, at least the direction for a solution is to be found in the understanding of 'New Israel' as the Old Testament's witness to reality. Jesus Christ is in the Old Testament in the sense that 'New Israel' is in the Old Testament. Whenever Israel responded in faith, the new existence, which is Jesus Christ, was taking tangible shape. For this reason the New Testament identifies appearances of the new life in Israel's history with Jesus Christ. Abraham saw Christ's day (John 8.56); Moses suffered for Christ's sake (Heb. 11.26); Isaiah saw his glory and spoke of him (John 12.41).

The great challenge to Old Testament scholarship in our time is to retain and extend our vast knowledge of Israel's total life, which has been opened up by historical research, while at the same time to use this understanding in such a way as to recover the Old Testament for the Christian Church.

INDEX OF AUTHORS

INDEX OF REFERENCES

Ref.	Page	Ref.	Page	Ref.	Page
OLD TESTAMENT		9.2	55	12.25	34
		14.1	51	18.18	34
Genesis		26.5 ff.	78	38.7	50
1–2	31–43	32.5	57	38.17	34
1–2.4a	32	32.10	33	*Psalms*	
2	95	32.11	34	29.1	50
3	32, 36, 40	*Joshua*		46.6	86
5	39	5.2	61	48.3	86, 88
7	39	15.14	55	49.20	34
14–15	39	*Judges*		50.2	86
16–17	39	9.37	86	51.12	79
20	39	11.34 ff.	65	68.17	86
21	39	*I Samuel*		78.68	86
4b ff.	32, 37	10.10	35	78.69	86
10–14	88	11.14	79	87.2	86
1–5	43–50, 95, 97	26.19	51	88.13	34
6	46	*II Samuel*		89.7	50
8	35	6.1 ff.	90, 91	103.5	79
1–4	50–59, 97	*I Kings*		104.30	79
1	35	20.35	51	125.1	86
2	34	*II Kings*		132.13–14	86
.1 ff.	63	18.4	47	*Isaiah*	
.1 ff.	65	*I Chronicles*		2.2 ff.	87, 88
.2	86	21.18	86	6.1 ff.	83
.14	86	22.1	91	6.2	61
.10–22	65	*II Chronicles*		7.20	61
.22 ff.	60	3.1	86, 91	10.26	78
Exodus		7.1 ff.	86	11.1–9	65
23	61	15.8	79	11.6–9	65–69, 77, 87
19	59, 61	24.4	79	14.1–23	71
20	59, 61	*Esther*		14.12–21	69–72
24–26	49, 65	1.13	76	14.13	86, 89
.17	86	*Job*		24.10	33
Numbers		1.6	50	27.1	38
.33	55	2.1	50	28.14 ff.	92
.9	47			28.16	86
..2	35			29.21	33
Deuteronomy				30.7	37
28	55			32.15	66, 88